BUILDING REAL
FURNITURE
FOR EVERYDAY LIFE

BY CHRIS GLEASON

POPULAR WOODWORKING BOOKS
CINCINNATI, OHIO
www.popularwoodworking.com

To prevent accidents, keep safety in mind while you work. Use the safety guards installed on power equipment; they are for your protection. When working on power equipment, keep fingers away from saw blades, wear safety goggles to prevent injuries from flying wood chips and sawdust, wear ear protection and consider installing a dust vacuum to reduce the amount of airborne sawdust in your woodshop. Don't wear loose clothing, such as neckties or shirts with loose sleeves, or jewelry, such as rings, necklaces or bracelets, when working on power equipment. Tie back long hair to prevent it from getting caught in equipment. People who are sensitive to certain chemicals should check the chemical content of any product before using it. The authors and editors who compiled this book have tried to make the contents as accurate and correct as possible. Plans, il-lustrations, photographs and text have been carefully checked. All instructions, plans and projects should be carefully read, studied and understood before beginning construction. Due to the variability of local conditions, construction materials, skill levels, etc., neither the author nor Popular Woodworking Books assumes any responsibility for any accidents, injuries, damages or other losses incurred resulting from the material presented in this book. Prices listed for supplies and equipment were current at the time of publication and are subject to change. Glass shelving should have all edges polished and must be tempered. Untempered glass shelves may shatter and can cause serious bodily injury. Tempered shelves are very strong and if they break will just crumble, minimizing personal injury.

BUILDING REAL FURNITURE FOR EVERYDAY LIFE. Copyright © 2006 by Chris Gleason. Printed in Singapore. All rights reserved. No part of this book may be reproduced in any form or by any electronic or mechanical means including information storage and retrieval systems without permission in writing from the publisher, except by a reviewer, who may quote brief passages in a review. Published by Popular Woodworking Books, an imprint of F&W Publications, Inc., 4700 East Galbraith Road, Cincinnati, Ohio, 45236. First edition.

Distributed in Canada by Fraser Direct
100 Armstrong Avenue
Georgetown, Ontario L7G 5S4
Canada

Distributed in the U.K. and Europe by David & Charles
Brunel House
Newton Abbot
Devon TQ12 4PU
England
Tel: (+44) 1626 323200
Fax: (+44) 1626 323319
E-mail: mail@davidandcharles.co.uk

Distributed in Australia by Capricorn Link
P.O. Box 704
Windsor, NSW 2756
Australia

Visit our Web site at www.popularwoodworking.com for information on more resources for woodworkers.

Other fine Popular Woodworking Books are available from your local bookstore or direct from the publisher.

10   09   08   07   06   5   4   3   2   1

Library of Congress Cataloging-in-Publication Data

Gleason, Chris, 1973-
    Building real furniture for everyday life / Chris Gleason.
        p.   cm.
    Includes index.
    ISBN 1-55870-760-3 (pbk: alk. paper)
    ISBN 1-55870-780-8 (hardcover: alk. paper)
    1. Furniture making.   2. Woodwork — Patterns.   I. Title.
TT194.G54   2006
684.1'04--dc22   2005016535

Metric Conversion Chart

TO CONVERT	TO	MULTIPLY BY
Inches	Centimeters	2.54
Centimeters	Inches	0.4
Feet	Centimeters	30.5
Centimeters	Feet	0.03
Yards	Meters	0.9
Meters	Yards	1.1

Acquisitions editor: Jim Stack
Editor: Amy Hattersley
Cover Design: Brian Roeth
Design/Page Layout: Amy Wilkin/Dragonfly Graphics, LLC
Project photographer: Paul B. Richer
Technical illustrator: Hayes Shanesy
Production coordinator: Jennifer L. Wagner

F+W PUBLICATIONS, INC.

about the author

A self-taught woodworker, Chris Gleason has operated Gleason Woodworking Studio for more than seven years. Although he started out as a fairly inexperienced woodworker, he persevered to become an expert in contemporary furniture design and construction. Learning mostly through trial and error, he devoured every woodworking book and magazine that he could get his hands on; with this in mind, he sincerely hopes to pass along some useful techniques and concepts to aspiring furniture makers.

With a degree in French from Vassar College in Poughkeepsie, New York, Chris also studied abroad for a year in Switzerland. When he's not in the shop, he enjoys mountain biking and skiing near his home in Salt Lake City, Utah, and playing old-time banjo and fiddle.

acknowledgements

I am grateful to my wife, Michele, for her patience, especially early on, before the business gained momentum and took on a life of its own. I also wish to thank my father, a small businessman himself, and my mother, for their support and encouragement.

table of
CONTENTS

INTRODUCTION

the *purpose of this book* is to present contemporary furniture projects for beginning and intermediate woodworkers who seek techniques, plans and inspiration for building simple, sturdy furniture they'll use in their own homes.

In the spirit of keeping projects within the skill level and tooling constraints of most hobbyist woodworkers, I have designed durable furniture using straightforward methods of construction. When it comes to joinery, for example, I am a great fan of pocket screws and biscuits for both their installation speed and strength. For those who are interested, of course, it is always possible to employ more complicated methods. Hand-cut dovetails, for example, are lovely when skillfully crafted and would lend strength and beauty to a number of projects in this book, but detailing their execution is beyond the scope of this text. Most of the projects you'll find here can be completed within a few hours.

Some people take great pleasure in complex tool setups and layouts, while others would rather watch a project come together quickly and make its way into the house as soon as possible. To minimize construction time, I have chosen not only techniques but also materials that simplify the construction process. For instance, I frequently rely on easy-to-use veneered plywoods instead of solid lumber, which must be joined, planed and glued up, then planed (or sanded) again. You'll find nearly all the materials necessary for these projects at home centers and hardware stores. A listing of some preferred suppliers is included in the back of the book, and the Internet provides access to a vast selection of innovative products at great prices — if you know where to look.

Best wishes,

Chris Gleason

green
DESIGN

environmentally-friendly consumer goods are getting a lot of press these days — even the most mainstream magazines and catalogs are featuring more and more "green" products. While I'll be the first to admit that I don't use green products 100 percent of the time, I do believe that woodworkers can collectively produce positive results by making wise choices. You can embrace green design in a number of ways including, but not limited to, the following.

RECYCLED MATERIALS

Architectural salvage yards: The city I live in (and many others, I'm sure) has a fantastic architectural salvage yard, which often features hard and soft wood lumber as well as all kinds of "you'll know it when you see it" treasures. I recently built a bed with a frame and panel headboard, the panel of which came from an old maple door.

Lumber reclaimers: A lot of companies reclaim lumber from old buildings and mill it for use in furniture and cabinetry. The wood is often expensive, but there are some bargains to be had.

Kirei board: Made from stalks of the sorghum plant compressed into panels, these boards are used like you would plywood or particleboard.

Woodstalk/Wheatboard: Recycled wheat hulls, which are ordinarily a waste product, are pressed into panels that resemble particleboard and can be used as such. The adhesives are formaldehyde-free, and you can buy it with melamine laminated to the sides for cabinetry.

LOW & NO VOC FINISHING PRODUCTS

Finishing is one of the areas where woodworkers can make a big difference — and it is immediately observable! Open a can of lacquer and take a whiff (on second thought, don't, it makes a lot of people nauseated). Then compare with the newer water-based urethanes, which are almost odorless. You can take it a step further and use Tried & True

linseed oil finishes, which are made only of beeswax and linseed oil — they smell so good you'll want to eat them right out of the can (don't do that either). The point is, there are choices when it comes to finishing products and some are definitely safer than others, so choose wisely. Not only are there many more pleasant finishes available to use, they also will not release harmful VOCs in the future.

Companies to check out:
- BioShield Paints (www.bioshieldpaint.com)
- AURO (www.aurousa.com)
- America's Pride
- Tried & True Wood Finishes (www.triedandtruewoodfinish.com)
- Minwax (www.minwax.com)
- Homestead Finishing Products (TransTint Dyes) (www.homesteadfinishing.com)
- Zinsser (Bulls Eye Shellac) (www.zinsser.com)

SUSTAINABLY-HARVESTED MATERIALS

Bamboo: Fast-growing and long-lived, timber bamboo grows to a height of 40' (1219mm) with a diameter exceeding 6" (152m), and it matures in 4 years. Bamboo is a grass. From an environmental standpoint, that's important: Unlike traditional hardwoods, bamboo does not require replanting when harvested. Mature bamboo has an extensive root system that continues to send up new shoots for decades. It is grown in managed forests, and harvesting is done by hand, minimizing the impact on the local environment. By working with bamboo and understanding its growth patterns, bamboo farmers are able to maximize timber production and maintain healthy forests.

Smart Wood: The Forest Stewardship Council (FSC) is an independent organization that audits the harvesting and stewardship practices of timber suppliers worldwide. Some home centers have committed to the purchase and retail of FSC-certified lumber products, which are managed and harvested under strict guidelines to ensure that sustainable practices are followed. Some certified timber can be tracked through its entire journey from stump to shelf.

FINISHING 101

f *inishing is tricky because* it can make or break a project. The typical conundrum is that most of us spend most of our time and energy on the construction aspect of a project, so by the time we're ready to apply the finish, we've run out of gas and just want to get it over with as quickly as possible. High-end professional furniture makers will often plan for 30% of their time to be spent finishing — a high standard to meet for most of us. I have experimented with everything under the sun at this point, and have made mistakes and learned a great deal about what works and what doesn't. Here I'll attempt to summarize what I've learned so that you can create beautiful and durable finishes as easily and quickly as possible. Bear in mind, however, that finishing is an extremely subjective process, what one person finds ideal may not satisfy someone else, so in the beginning, keep an open mind and see what works for you.

My primary recommendation for clear-coat finishes: water-based polyurethanes. I use them almost exclusively because they are easy to apply, are very durable and are a pleasure to work with — almost no odor at all. They are also extremely fast-drying under normal conditions, I can apply three coats in an afternoon, which is critical in a commercial context and pretty handy in a more casual environment, too.

Sand between coats: depending on how much the grain has raised, I use either 220, 320, 400 or 600 grit between coats. This may sound like shades of grey but believe me, the nuances make a difference. Keep in mind that auto-body finish-

ers use 2000g paper in their work, and after a while you will start to regard 180g as shockingly coarse. In my experience, you may not have to sand between every coat—maybe just after the first, depending on how the finish goes on. I use a ¼ sheet palm sander for this, and it is very quick, so don't worry that you're adding much tedium to the process. It is fast, and well worth it.

For a soft, waxy finish that is a pleasure to touch, you might try wet-sanding your final coat with 600g paper and mineral oil. I use an ordinary palm sander for this, and wipe off the excess with a paper towel. A word to the wise: this may get messy, so wear old clothes, but the result is generally worth it.

In general, I insist on hardware store foam brushes, which some consider heretical but I stand by my results. They are disposable, which makes them easy to deal with, and they apply paints, stains and polyurethanes in a nice, uniform manner. I also find that their chisel tips are great for getting into corners. For both environmental and economical reasons, I am very careful about using them for as long as possible: by simply wrapping them in a plastic bag between uses, I can actually go a couple of weeks on a single 4" (102mm) wide foam brush, depending on what I'm brushing on. Some folks go the extra mile and store the wrapped brushes in the fridge, but if you do, make sure the wrapping is tight or they will actually tend to dry out quicker.

Ventilation is key, although much less so for the water-based products out there. If you can, it doesn't hurt to have a fan running and/or open doors and windows.

For large interior projects that will be painted on-site, I recommend low VOC

(volatile organic compounds) from America's Pride. They are almost odorless, and are great for use anyplace where people and pets will spend time.

Water-based stains can be tough to apply: they dry very quickly, so you need to be on your toes. I also have a tough time getting the colors to be as deep and rich as I'd like — this is largely because they work by sitting on top of the wood rather than penetrating deeply and refracting light within it.

My favorite method for staining wood is to use the TransTint pigments (see the Resources section of this book) for water soluble dyes. A small container goes a long way, and they are a complete breeze to apply. No fumes, completely even penetration and very forgiving on pretty much everything I've used them on. There are a number of colors available, plus you can mix and match to your heart's content. I have used them many times for helping to match antique finishes with great success.

Oil finishes appeal to a lot of people because they are easy to use — just flood and wipe — and they do bring out the grain beautifully in most species. However, most oil finishes do not provide much durability, and some need to be reapplied annually. Any places where water is concerned (i.e. kitchen and bathroom cabinets), I don't advise using them. The one exception is for butcherblock countertops which are designed to be cut on, I like Tried & True varnish oil, which is a polymerized oil and beeswax blend. It builds up a nice thick body but requires many coats at first and occasional re-coating from then on. There might be some other good oils out there, but overall they aren't my area of expertise.

blanket
CHEST

Veneered plywood comes to the rescue in my quest for maximum effect at minimal cost. Not only is this material cost-effective, I also was able to design the chest in such a way that you need only one 4' × 8' (122cm × 244cm) sheet to get the job done. The dimensions I initially planned for, based on my earliest sketches, required a second sheet, so I made a few modifications in size and scale that don't compromise the finished piece at all. Feel free to make any changes you'd like in your own version, but be forewarned: The chest can't get any bigger without requiring more materials!

This piece is a fun variation on a theme I affectionately call "case on a base." In essence, you build a large box and set it on a reinforced base that has enough detail to be interesting. The lid sits on top of the box and is attached with two 4"-long (102mm) butt hinges. I had originally planned to use a piano hinge, but the ¾"-thick (19mm) top turned out to be plenty rigid on its own. The piano hinge would have been overkill (and you also save about $10 by forgoing it).

I have a real thing for exposed plywood edges, and in this case they serve double-duty as both a time-saver and an important design element. I originally planned to edge-band them, but I realized that blending them in would diminish the piece's visual interest. The strong vertical lines at the corners of the chest and along the edge of the lid are details that make the piece a lot more interesting than it would be otherwise. They also reinforce the color contrast that occurs between the painted chest and the clear-coated base.

project drawing top, front, elevation

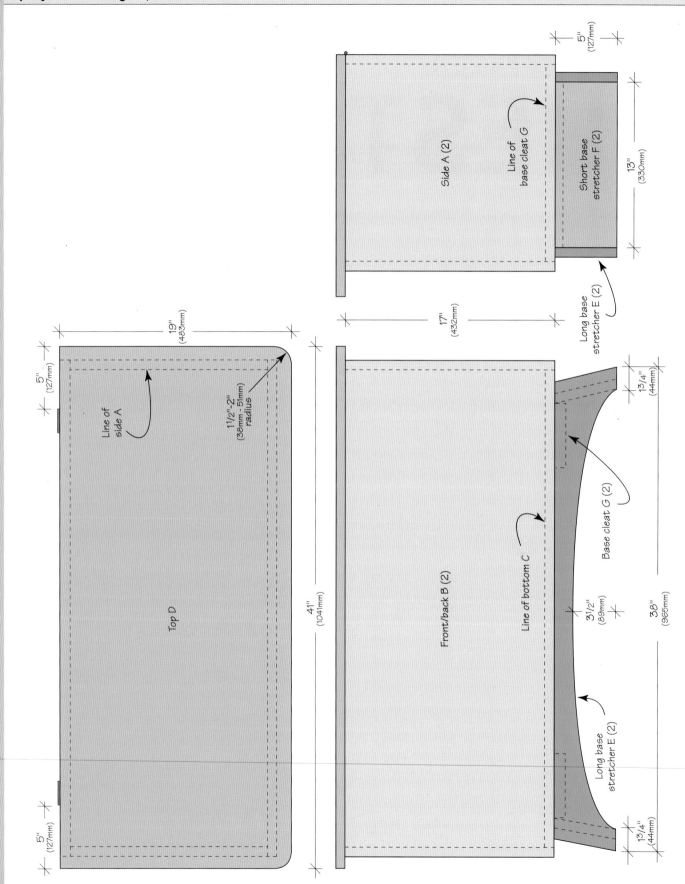

Top D

Line of side A

5" (127mm)

19" (483mm)

1 1/2"-2" (38mm - 51mm) radius

41" (1041mm)

Side A (2)

Line of base cleat G

5" (127mm)

Short base stretcher F (2)

13" (330mm)

Long base stretcher E (2)

17" (432mm)

Front/back B (2)

Line of bottom C

Base cleat G (2)

Long base stretcher E (2)

3 1/2" (89mm)

1 3/4" (44mm)

1 3/4" (44mm)

38" (965mm)

cutting list inches (millimeters)

REFERENCE	QUANTITY	PART	STOCK	THICKNESS	(mm)	WIDTH	(mm)	LENGTH	(mm)
A	2	sides	veneered plywood	¾	(19)	17	(432)	17	(432)
B	2	front & back	veneered plywood	¾	(19)	17	(432)	39	(991)
C	1	bottom	veneered plywood	¾	(19)	17	(432)	37½	(953)
D	1	top	veneered plywood	¾	(19)	19	(483)	41	(1041)
E	2	base long stretchers	veneered plywood	¾	(19)	5	(127)	38	(965)
F	2	base short stretchers	veneered plywood	¾	(19)	5	(127)	13	(330)
G	2	base top stretchers	veneered plywood	¾	(19)	5	(127)	13	(330)

hardware & supplies

- 30-40 1¼" (32mm) screws for pocket holes

- 2 4"-long (102mm) butt hinges (non-removable pin)

step 1 ■ Step one is straightforward. Using a table saw or circular saw and a straightedge, cut out the parts for the chest itself: a pair of sides, a matching front and back and a bottom. I used ¾" (19mm) plywood for the bottom because I figured the chest might hold some heavy stuff in the future, and I wanted the bottom to be plenty strong.

step 2 ■ I used pocket screws to assemble this project, but biscuits are another appropriate choice. If you decide to use biscuits, follow the same basic series of construction steps, but allow some time in between steps 5 and 6 for the glue to dry. I begin by cutting the pocket holes on the bottom side of the bottom panel and proceed to cut the holes on all four sides.

step 3 ■ Drill pocket holes into the two side panels, on their inside face, at the front and back edges.

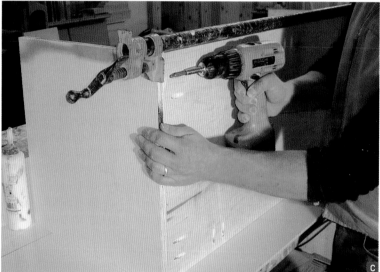

step 4 ■ Assemble the sides and bottom to form a U shape. I do this with the parts positioned on the bench in such a way to give me easy access to the pocket holes (imagine the chest assembled and tipped onto its back). Start with just one side at a time: it's easier than trying to clamp the whole thing up perfectly all at once. Apply a thin bead of glue and wipe the excess with a damp rag right away. Place a clamp across the top edge, screw in the top corner, then move the clamp lower down the assembly and align and screw in the bottom corner. Secure the screws in between, and do the opposing side in the same manner.

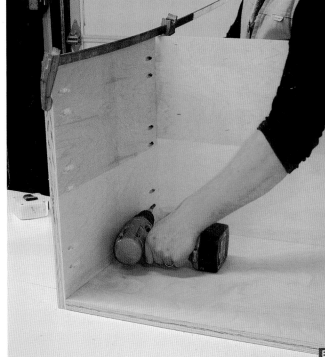

step 5 ■ To continue the assembly, clamp the front panel into place and fasten it through the pocket holes from the inside and bottom. Then repeat with the back panel: The result is a finished box.

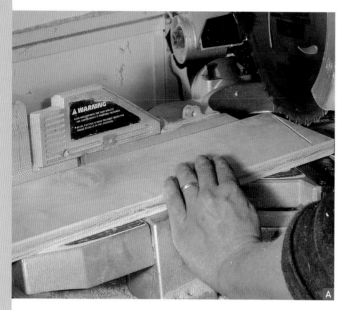

step 6 ■ Rip parts for the base. On the long stretchers, you'll need to cut the ends so they taper upward at 15°. I set the blade to 15° on my crosscut saw and make the cuts. The finished length of the long stretchers at the widest point should be 36" (914mm).

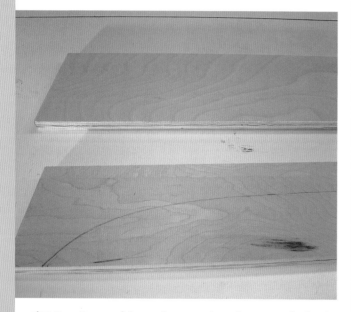

step 7 ■ On one of the two long stretchers, draw an arc freehand across half of the stretcher. The arc begins at 1¾" (45mm) from the bottom corner, and at its highest point, it rises to 3½" (89mm) high. This is not a geometrically derived arc. Simply draw a pleasing curve that is even and looks nice.

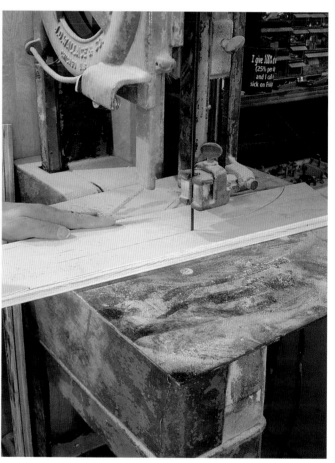

step 8 ■ On the band saw (or with a hand-held jigsaw), cut out the arc. When you get to the halfway point, stop cutting. Now make a cut at the center and at a right angle to the bottom of the arc blank up to the cut you just made.to remove the waste material. Flip over this waste piece and use it as a template to trace the remaining half of the arch.

step 9 ■ Trace the arc on the other half of the stretcher and cut it out.

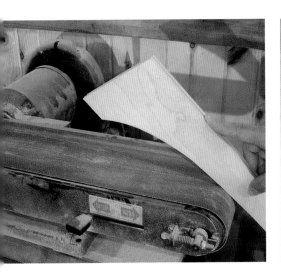

step 10 ■ If you work carefully, your cuts will be clean, but sanders will make quick work of any irregularities.

step 11 ■ You can now use the first stretcher as a template for the second.

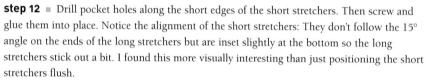

step 12 ▪ Drill pocket holes along the short edges of the short stretchers. Then screw and glue them into place. Notice the alignment of the short stretchers: They don't follow the 15° angle on the ends of the long stretchers but are inset slightly at the bottom so the long stretchers stick out a bit. I found this more visually interesting than just positioning the short stretchers flush.

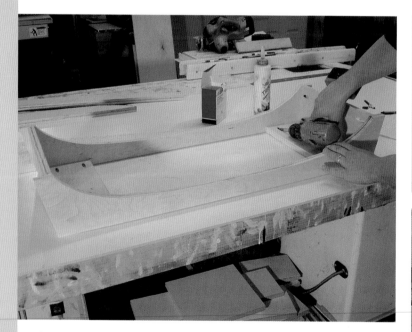

step 13 ▪ The base top stretchers install easily if you position the base upside down on the bench.

step 14 ▪ The base screws directly onto the bottom of the chest — simply center it side-to-side and front-to-back.

step 15 ■ The lid is a little tricky to attach, but it isn't rocket science, either. First, position the hinges on the back edge of the chest, about 5" (127mm) in from each side, and screw them down. Then place the lid on the chest and mark the hinge locations on the back edge of the lid. Set the lid on your bench, upside down, and transfer the marks onto the underside of the lid. With the hinges unscrewed from the chest, place them on the underside of the lid and screw them down, using only one hole in case there is a misalignment and you have to redo this. At this point, carry the lid back over to the chest and screw the hinges into the predrilled holes. The alignment should be perfect, so go ahead and screw the lid on. If the lid doesn't line up properly, fixing it should be fairly intuitive: Remove a screw as needed, position the lid in the right spot and screw down the hinge right there. You'll notice that the lid is centered on the chest side-to-side but not front to back. This is so you can place the chest almost flush against a wall or a bed and open it without the back edge of the lid bumping into anything.

step 16 ■ The front corners of the lid get rounded over — to make the curved edges, use an object that has the desired radius or use a compass if you're so inclined. A jigsaw will quickly round them over. A round edge is practical in that it keeps clothing from snagging and legs from getting impaled, and it is aesthetic in that it produces a more refined feel.

mobile file
CABINET

One of my favorite custom furniture clients was a hip graphic design firm located in a funky old warehouse in Madison, Wisconsin. Because the employees often invited their clients into their office, their furnishings needed to communicate their good taste and design savvy. To fit in with their contemporary, industrial space, they wanted a modern, minimalist file cabinet. Fortunately, my no-frills design also helped keep the budget reasonable — a critical consideration since they needed to order 40 cabinets.

The final design is a real triumph of simplicity — a plywood box on casters, with two smaller plywood boxes mounted inside on drawer slides. Many finishing schemes are possible, but I think that the design works especially well when you use contrasting finishing elements such as paint, stain or clear varnish on its various components. In this case, I chose a muted green for the cabinet and battleship gray for the drawers.

You can build the cabinet box several ways, depending on your tools, experience and schedule. I built the prototype with countersunk through-screws because I liked the exposed screw heads, but I assembled all of the final versions with biscuits, as the client preferred the cleaner look of hidden joinery. If you own a pocket hole jig, and I hope you do, you can use it to quickly assemble the cabinet with hidden joints. Regardless of the joinery method used, I recommend a ¾" (19mm) plywood back, because it's likely that even a small file cabinet will be expected to hold a lot of weight. I would hate to see the file cabinet start to slouch sideways over time. The cost increase is negligible, especially for the durability that it provides.

I built this file cabinet to fit underneath a desktop, but you can easily modify the design to improve its utility. For example, you can build the cabinet taller, with three or four vertically stacked file drawers. Or stretch it out wider to make a four or even six drawer unit. And depending on your own needs, you might substitute two or three shorter drawers for a large one.

project drawing top, front, elevation

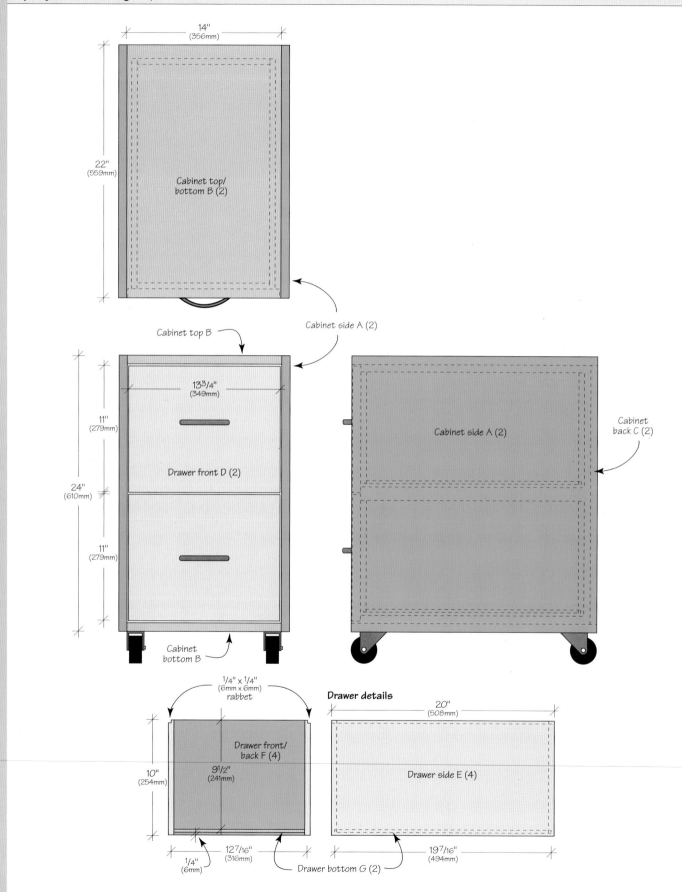

14"
(356mm)

22"
(559mm)

Cabinet top/
bottom B (2)

Cabinet top B

Cabinet side A (2)

13³/4"
(349mm)

11"
(279mm)

Drawer front D (2)

24"
(610mm)

11"
(279mm)

Cabinet
bottom B

Cabinet side A (2)

Cabinet
back C (2)

1/4" x 1/4"
(6mm x 6mm)
rabbet

Drawer details

20"
(508mm)

Drawer front/
back F (4)

10"
(254mm)

9¹/2"
(241mm)

Drawer side E (4)

1/4"
(6mm)

12⁷/16"
(316mm)

19⁷/16"
(494mm)

Drawer bottom G (2)

cutting list inches (millimeters)

REFERENCE	QUANTITY	PART	STOCK	THICKNESS	(mm)	WIDTH	(mm)	LENGTH	(mm)
A	2	cabinet sides	veneered plywood	¾	(19)	22	(559)	24	(610)
B	2	cabinet top & bottom	veneered plywood	¾	(19)	14	(356)	22	(559)
C	1	cabinet back	veneered plywood	¾	(19)	14	(356)	22½	(572)
D	2	drawer fronts	veneered plywood	¾	(19)	13¾	(349)	11	(279)
E	4	drawer sides	baltic birch plywood	½	(13)	10	(254)	20	(508)
F	4	drawer fronts & backs	baltic birch plywood	½	(13)	10	(254)	12	(305)
G	2	drawer bottoms	veneered plywood	¼	(6)	12⁷⁄₁₆	(316)	39⁷⁄₁₆	(1002)

hardware & supplies

- 2 pairs 20"-long (508mm) Accuride style ball-bearing drawer slides
- 2 drawer pulls
- 30-40 ¼" (6mm) screws for cabinet and drawer assembly
- 4 3" (76mm) diameter wheel casters (with mounting plates, not stems)
- 16 #10 panhead sheet metal screws
- 16 #10 flat washers

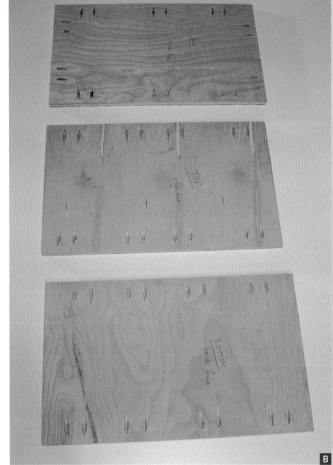

step 1 ■ The logical place to start is with the cabinet itself. Build this simple box to the specific dimensions provided in the materials list. You'll need to cut two identical side panels, a matching top and bottom, and a back. I used pocket screws for the joinery, note which panels get holes drilled and in which locations. Label the parts, using a pencil, on the inside faces of the panels to eliminate any confusion in the heat of the moment. With a simple piece like this, doing so isn't critical but it is a good habit to get into.

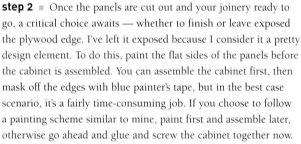

step 2 ■ Once the panels are cut out and your joinery ready to go, a critical choice awaits — whether to finish or leave exposed the plywood edge. I've left it exposed because I consider it a pretty design element. To do this, paint the flat sides of the panels before the cabinet is assembled. You can assemble the cabinet first, then mask off the edges with blue painter's tape, but in the best case scenario, it's a fairly time-consuming job. If you choose to follow a painting scheme similar to mine, paint first and assemble later, otherwise go ahead and glue and screw the cabinet together now.

Painting the panels prior to assembly is a snap. It is easy to be precise and fast, which is an unusual luxury. I recommend a 4"-wide (102mm) foam brush, because it is lays down a smooth coat of paint and is easy to control at the edges of the panels. Paint quickly, applying three thin coats. If necessary, sand with 320-grit paper between coats but not after the final coat. With a little practice, you'll be able to paint the panels without getting any drips on the edges (put just enough paint on the brush). In the meantime, you'll find it easy to sand drips once they're dry.

step 3 ■ While you're waiting for the paint to dry (it doesn't take long if you use thin coats), you can screw the casters onto the bottom side of the bottom panel. I use a beefy No.10 screw with a washer.

step 4 ▪ Once the paint is dry, assembly can begin in earnest. Lay one of the side panels down with its inside facing up, and set the bottom panel on top of it in preparation for being screwed down. If you aren't comfortable assembling cabinets with pocket holes, use a clamp. The parts tend to wander a bit when you apply the pressure necessary to drive screws.

Attach the top in the same manner, then drop the back in. Again, use clamps to ensure optimal alignment. When it comes time to attach the remaining side, flip the cabinet over onto that side — doing so is easier than standing on your head to drive screws upward. Using gravity in your favor is obvious when you see it done, but it took me a while to figure out initially.

(In the piece illustrated, I used a scrap of plywood that I had previously stained black on one side — it has nothing to do with this design, just my way of putting a perfectly good piece of wood to work.)

step 5 ▪ Use Accuride-style slides for this project. They are easy to install if you follow this method, which I learned through hours and hours of trial and error. Mount the slides in the cabinet first (I used a 4" (102mm) wide spacer to position the slides evenly), making sure you inset the slides ¾" (19mm) from the front of the cabinet. Once the slides are in place, screw them down with ⅝" (16mm) screws. Use the same spacer at the top and bottom of the cabinet. Extend the slides to access the mounting holes. When you've done one side, flip over the cabinet and repeat on the other side.

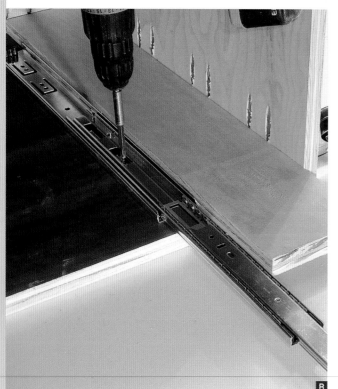

step 6 ■ The drawers are simple boxes with bottoms that are held inside a ¼"-deep (6mm) groove. Begin by cutting the plywood to size for the drawer sides, then rip the groove for the bottom using the table saw or router table. If you use the table saw, you could fit it with a dado blade, but for just a few pieces like this, I find that it isn't worth taking the time to swap blades. Instead make two side-by-side cuts totaling a ¼"-wide (6mm) groove. And make sure the groove is cut ¼" (6mm) from the bottom edge of the drawer.

TIP ■ drawer slides

Spend the money necessary to buy quality drawer slides that slide smoothly, even when handling a heavy load. A filled file drawer is heavy, and full-extension slides (rated at 75 lbs. per pair) are much more appropriate than the flimsier ones you often see. Not all home centers carry excellent quality slides, but most do, and any good wood-working store should. Full-extension slides enable you to pull the drawer all the way out. Most cheaper slides are three-quarter extension at best, and that isn't much of a selling point.

step 7 ■ Here's a simple solution for hanging file folders: Simply cut a rabbet on the top of the drawer sides. Cut the rabbet with a router table, or make two passes over the table saw. For the first pass, run the stock on its edge, then rotate it 90° and make a pass with the stock held flat on the table. The files can be hung on the lips created by cutting the rabbets.

step 9 ■ You'll assemble the drawers like you did the cabinet. Glue the bottom of the drawer into place as well — the plywood won't expand and contract, and the drawer will gain a lot of rigidity. Once the drawers are assembled, you can finish the interiors with a clearcoat of your choice: I recommend water-based polyurethane because it has little odor (you don't want a whiff of finishing product to waft out and hit you in the face every time you open a drawer).

step 8 ■ The drawers are held together with glue and pocket screws. Drill the pocket holes on the fronts and backs of the drawers. This way, the screws are hidden once the finished drawer fronts go on. Remember to adjust the stop collar on your pocket hole jig to accommodate the ½"-thick (13mm) plywood.

TIP ■ grain orientation

Grain orientation doesn't matter if you're building a piece out of a veneered plywood and you plan to paint it. Because plywood doesn't expand or contract the way solid wood does, you can orient it however you want without adjusting for seasonal movement caused by humidity changes in the environment. I mention this because I sometimes have scraps of plywood whose grain is going "the wrong way". But that's OK for a painted piece, and it is a good way to efficiently use materials.

step 10 ▪ It's easy to install the drawers at this point. Prepare the file cabinet to receive the drawers, insert a pair of ½"-thick (13mm) shims at the bottom and extend the slides a couple of inches. Set the drawer directly on the shims, flush up the tips of the slides with the front of the drawer, and screw the slides on through the front mounting holes. Pull the drawer out and screw in the back and middle holes as well. As long as you keep the drawer level while you're putting in the screws, it will move smoothly when the shims are removed and its front will be aligned with the front face of the cabinet. Adjust discrepancies by removing a screw and tilting the front or back edge of the drawer up or down, then re-screw to hold it in the new position. This will become obvious once you try it.

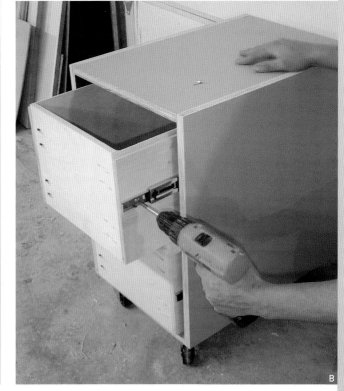

step 11 ▪ To install the top drawer, put 1"-thick (25mm) shims on the top edges of the bottom drawer, set the top drawer on these shims and repeat the process you just used for the bottom drawer.

step 12 ■ To attach the drawer fronts, first remove the top drawer so you have room to work. I prepainted the drawer fronts because I find it quicker and easier to do. To properly align the drawer fronts, use ⅛" (3mm) shims underneath the drawer front. They'll create a nice, even reveal, then center the drawer front side-to-side so the gap is even on both sides. Clamp it into place, then fasten it with from the inside with two 1"-long (25mm) screws.

TIP ■ drawer pulls

I used a simple template to help quickly and accurately mount drawer pulls. This is a good technique that can help out with other projects as well. Begin by cutting a scrap piece of wood that is the same width as the drawer front. The height is less important. In this case I wanted to position the pulls 5½" (140mm) from the top of the drawer front, so the template had to be just a bit longer than that. I just drew a horizontal line on the template at 5½" (140mm) from the top, and using a square, drew a vertical line perpendicular to it. The vertical line is in the center of the template. The holes on my pull measured 4" (102mm) apart, so I marked for holes to be drilled at 2" (51mm) from the left and right sides of the vertical centerline. I held my pull up to these marks as a common-sense check, then drilled the holes with a ³⁄₁₆" (5mm) bit. Though it takes time to make the template, you still save time because otherwise you would have to perform this process for every drawer pull you want to attach. On this two-drawer cabinet, you cut the time for mounting pulls in half. Imagine the savings when you have a whole kitchen full of drawers to tackle.

step 13 ▪ With the top drawer reinstalled, extend both drawers equally [about 6" (152mm) or so]. Place the ⅛" (3mm) shims on top of the bottom drawer front and set the top drawer front on it. Align it side-to-side, and clamp it into position. Screw it from the inside as before.

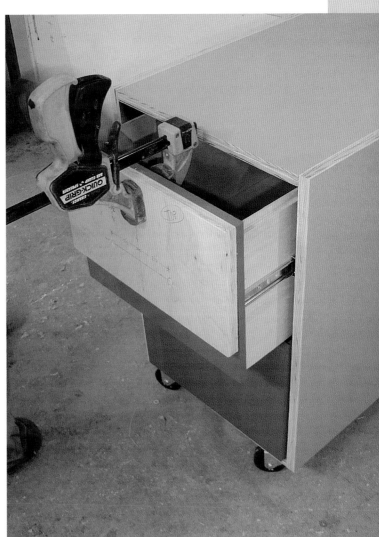

step 14 ▪ When I attach drawer pulls, I like to take my time drilling the holes. One wrong move means having to make a whole new drawer front, which is enough to keep me on my toes. Make a template (like the one I'm clamping to the drawer front in the photo) to prevent making mistakes on the finished cabinet. Drill the holes for the drawer pulls in the template and make sure they are spaced correctly. Also, locate the holes whatever distance down from the top of the drawer front you choose. To use the template, position it so it is centered on the drawer front and be sure the top of the template is flush with the top of the drawer front. Clamp it in place and drill the holes. Because this is a pull that I know I'll use on future projects, I'll save this template.

project three
DRESSER

this *dresser is so easy to build,* it almost feels like cheating. At its core, it is a bookcase planned around the dimensions of the plastic storage containers which serve as its drawers. With no hardware to purchase or install, it is also relatively inexpensive, especially if you can get a deal on the containers. Shop around; I found that prices varied quite a bit depending on the source. I also recommend purchasing the containers prior to building the dresser itself. This way, you can measure them exactly to ensure they fit perfectly into the finished piece.

In terms of joinery, I used pocket holes, but plugged screws are another good option. I found a deal on maple veneered plywood at my local home center. It has both a gorgeous figure and creamy white color, so I decided to finish it with a clear water-based polyurethane rather than cover it up with a stain or paint. I also elected to finish the parts prior to assembly, because it's easy to put on a smooth, even finish when you're dealing with a few flat panels. Finishing the piece once it is assembled isn't all that tough, but it does involve a lot of inside corners where varnish can pool up and drip, and some of those areas are pretty hard to reach. In my view, this project practically screams out for prefinishing: You'll save a lot of time and hassle, and will most likely end up with a much better result.

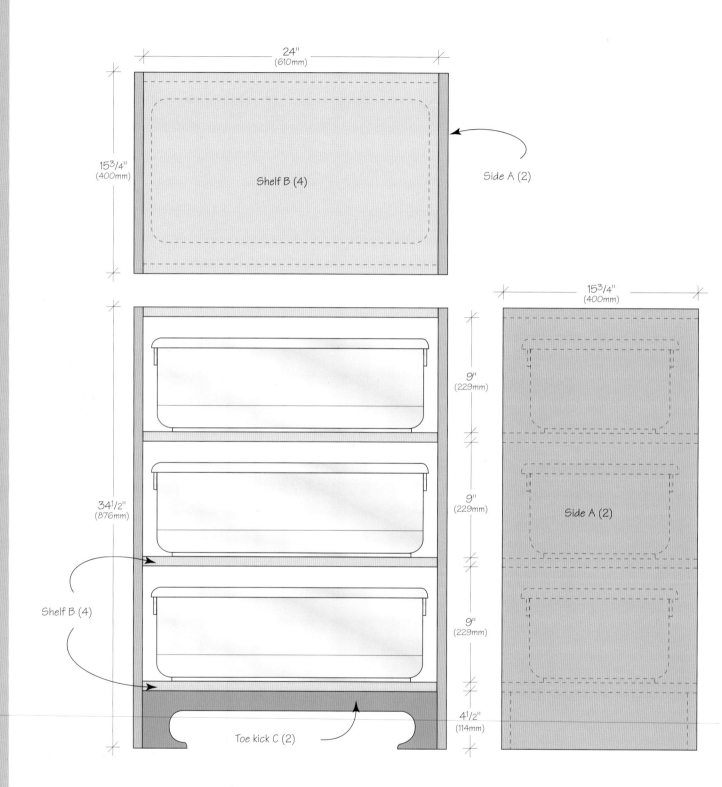

24"
(610mm)

15³/4"
(400mm)

Shelf B (4)

Side A (2)

15³/4"
(400mm)

9"
(229mm)

9"
(229mm)

34¹/2"
(876mm)

9"
(229mm)

Shelf B (4)

Side A (2)

4¹/2"
(114mm)

Toe kick C (2)

cutting list inches (millimeters)

REFERENCE	QUANTITY	PART	STOCK	THICKNESS	(mm)	WIDTH	(mm)	LENGTH	(mm)
A	2	sides	veneered plywood	¾	(19)	15¾	(400)	34½	(876)
B	4	shelves	veneered plywood	¾	(19)	15¾	(400)	24	(610)
C	2	toe-kicks	veneered plywood	¾	(19)	4½	(114)	24	(610)

hardware & supplies

▪ 3 clear plastic storage containers:
Sterilite 35 quart, 7" x 16" x 23" (178mm x 406mm x 584mm)

▪ 20-30 1¼" (32mm) screws for cabinet assembly

step 1 ▪ On the table saw, cut the panels to size. The dimensions in the cutting list reflect the size of the containers I used, so you'll need to modify them as necessary to suit your own purposes. My design calls for two identical side panels and four shelf panels. You can edge-band the panels if you like, but I am a big fan of the exposed plywood edge, so I left them uncovered.

step 2 ▪ As I mentioned earlier, prefinishing the panels prior to assembly saves a lot of time and headaches, so now is the time. Apply three coats of water-based polyurethane with a 4" (102mm) foam brush, and sand with 320-grit sandpaper between coats. Once the final coat is dry, sand very lightly, using almost no pressure at all, with 600-grit paper, just to pull out any last bumps.

step 3 ▪ You'll need to drill pocket holes into the shelf ends. I positioned the holes on the underside of the shelves so they are hidden.

step 4 ▪ Start with the top shelf, because it is easy to place accurately. Just align its top side with the upper edge of the side panel. Use a clamp to hold the panels in alignment while you drive the screws.

step 5 ■ Once the top shelf is affixed, cut a spacer to help position the lower shelves. I used containers of a uniform height, so I needed only one spacer to set the height for all of the shelves. If you have containers that vary in size, you'll need spacers that reflect these differences. In this case, my containers are about 7½" (191mm) high, so I used an 8"-wide (203mm) scrap of plywood for my spacer. This allows for clearance above each container for a nice fit. Using a spacer speeds up the assembly, and by using one, you won't have any pencil lines to erase or sand off later.

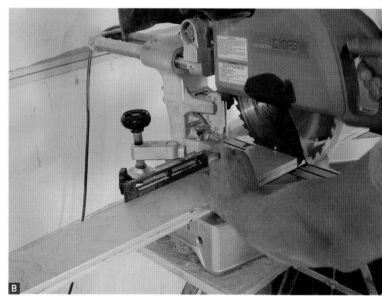

step 6 ■ The dresser features a 4" (102mm) opening beneath the bottom shelf. By filling in this opening with a tightly fitted panel (toe kick) on the back side of the dresser, the dresser gains considerable strength and is less likely to wobble from side-to-side. Pocket screws hold the panel in place.

step 7 ▪ The front side's fitted panel gets a cut out to add visual interest. To get ideas, check out the base designs in various other chapters in this book. You may also find inspiration in an antique or other piece that you already own. I traced the radius of a small can to create the curved shape of my design.

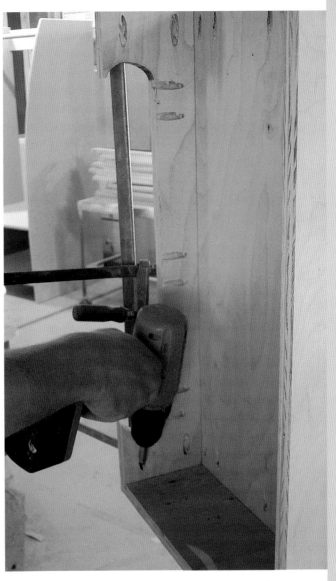

step 8 ▪ The front panel is attached with pocket screws.

step 9 ▪ Using the spacer, install the remaining side.

project four

ARMOIRE

running low on closet space? Who isn't? Here's a really quick
and useful solution. I used ¾"-thick (19mm) particleboard, but feel free to
substitute any type of panel you like. I considered oriented strand board (OSB),
the stuff that you see used on houses as exterior sheathing before the siding goes up,
because I like its raw, patchy look. But I had to admit it would look out of place in
my bedroom. If you have an industrial loft-type interior, however, it is a material
that might interest you.

Even though it is large, this armoire is one of the most quickly made projects
in the book, and for that reason alone, it's pretty satisfying to build. For the "cubby"
at the bottom, I decided to use a basket I already owned. You can do the same, or if
you don't have one, I'm sure you can find one without having to shop till you drop.
If you're inclined, you can also build a drawer instead. Check out the Mobile File
Cabinet project for ideas on drawer construction and tips on installing drawer slides.

Other nifty modifications include leaving the sides flat instead of curving them
toward the back, and adding doors to the large hanging area. If you decide to add
doors, install a top panel as well. You'll find tips for door fabrication and installation
in the Wall Cabinet project.

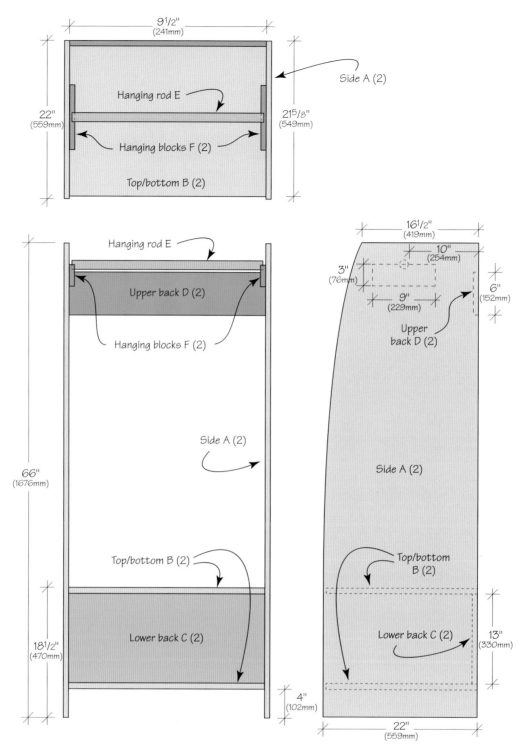

Side A (2)

9¹/₂"
(241mm)

22"
(559mm)

21⁵/₈"
(549mm)

Hanging rod E

Hanging blocks F (2)

Top/bottom B (2)

Hanging rod E

Upper back D (2)

Hanging blocks F (2)

Side A (2)

66"
(1676mm)

Top/bottom B (2)

Lower back C (2)

18¹/₂"
(470mm)

4"
(102mm)

16¹/₂"
(419mm)

10"
(254mm)

3"
(76mm)

9"
(229mm)

6"
(152mm)

Upper
back D (2)

Side A (2)

Top/bottom
B (2)

Lower back C (2)

13"
(330mm)

22"
(559mm)

cutting list inches (millimeters)

REFERENCE	QUANTITY	PART	STOCK	THICKNESS	(mm)	WIDTH	(mm)	LENGTH	(mm)
A	2	sides	particleboard	¾	(19)	23⁷/₈	(606)	66	(1676)
B	2	top & bottom	particleboard	¾	(19)	23	(584)	28½	(724)
C	1	lower back	particleboard	¾	(19)	13	(330)	28½	(724)
D	1	upper back	particleboard	¾	(19)	6	(152)	28½	(724)
E	1	hanging rod	hardwood	1¼	(32)	1¼	(32)	28½	(724)
F	2	hanging blocks	particleboard	¾	(19)	6	(152)	9	(229)

hardware & supplies

▪ 20 3" (76mm) galvanized deck screws for assembly

▪ 4 1¼" (32mm) drywall screws

▪ 1 basket or bin to fit into lower compartment (or leave the compartment open)

step 1 ∎ Begin this project by cutting out the two sides and two horizontal panels that you'll use as the top and bottom of the lower compartment. I used a 4' × 8' (1219mm × 2438mm) sheet of particleboard, which I ripped into two halves [hence the 23⅞" (606mm) width], but you could also purchase 24"-wide (610mm) panels, which are easier to haul around.

You'll note in the cutting list that the top and bottom panels are not as wide as the side panels. This is because they are inset from the front edge of the sides (due to the roundover on the panels). All will make sense to you when you line up the panels for assembly in step 7.

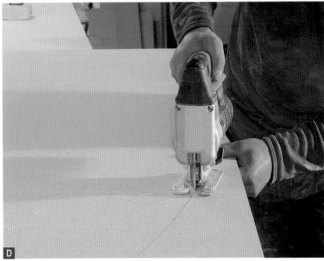

step 2 ∎ You can treat the sides in any number of ways: you can leave them as rectangular panels, or you could taper them back and up at an angle, or, as I chose to do here, you could curve them back and upward. Should you want to follow my example, refer to the sidebar in this chapter. To lay out the curve on the second side panel, I just traced the first side, which ensures that they're a consistent shape.

step 3 ▪ With a roundover bit in my router, I roundover the edges slightly. There are basically three reasons to do this:

Aesthetics: it looks a lot more finished
Safer: a sharp 90 degree particle board edge can actually cut you
More durable: a rounded-over edge won't chip out as a square one could

After routing, I recommend quickly sanding the edge by hand to produce a smooth bullnose.

laying out a curve
ON A FLAT PANEL

Here's one of my favorite methods for laying out a curve. You begin with a scrap of thin, flexible material, in this instance ⅛" (3mm) thick hardboard. The exact width of the strip doesn't matter [you'll note in the photos that I used a piece that was about 9" (229mm) wide], and the length isn't critical either — I'd make sure that it is about 12" (305mm) longer than the distance you'll be spanning.

You'll also need two small blocks of ¾" (19mm) thick scrap, about 4" x 4" (102mm x 102mm). These get screwed onto the backside of the strip, and you can then clamp these scrap blocks to your panel so that the desired curve is marked out by the strip. You'll need to know where the curve begins and ends

on the side panel: for the armoire, I suggest measuring about 16½" (419mm) from the back edge on the top of the side panel, and about 19" (483mm) up from the bottom edge. Make a couple of marks at these locations. Clamp one of the scrap blocks down so that the edge of the hardboard strip runs through one of the marks, and then line up the hardboard strip with the mark on the other end, and apply some pressure so that the strip curves into the shape you like. With the second end clamped into place, you can trace the outside edge of the curve, and then remove the hardboard strip. You're then ready to cut with a jigsaw or bandsaw, depending on the size of the workpiece. Any irregularities in the cut can usually be cleaned up quickly with a hand sander.

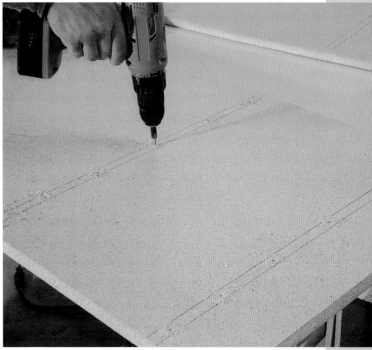

step 4 ■ To assure proper placement of the top and bottom panels, use a framing square to draw layout lines on the side panels. I drew a line 4" (102mm) up from the bottom edge, and another that is 17¾" (451mm) from the bottom edge. The upper line reflects the size of the opening I need for the basket I intend to place there, so modify this dimension according to your own needs. Then draw in lines ¾" (19mm) above these initial lines, clearly indicating where the top and bottom panels will fall.

step 5 ■ Join the panels with long screws. Between the lines, drill six pilot holes for each panel.

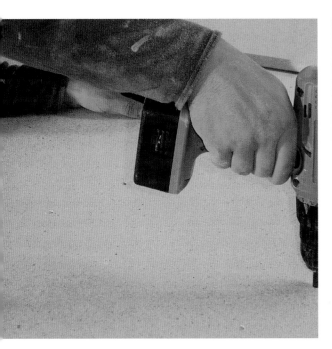

step 6 ■ Flip the panels over, and countersink the holes so the screw heads sit flush with the outside surface of the side panels.

step 7 ■ It's time for assembly, so clamp the bottom panel to one of the side panels; use the layout lines to simplify this task.

step 8 ■ Use 3" (76mm) galvanized decking screws to secure the bottom panel.

step 9 ■ Clamp and screw the top panel into position the same way.

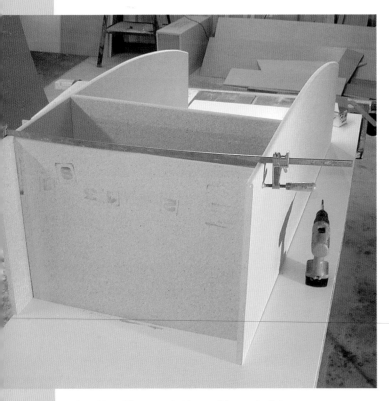

step 10 ■ The second side panel is attached the same way.

step 11 ■ The whole assembly gains strength when you insert a snug-fitting back panel into the lower compartment. Secure it with counter-sunk screws.

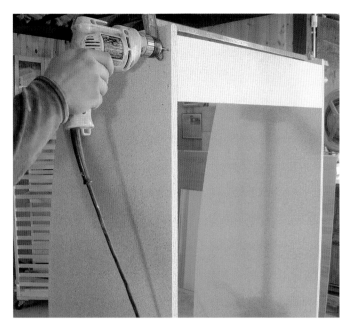

step 12 ■ To keep the armoire from racking (wobbling from side-to-side), make and install an upper stretcher near the top. The wider it is, the better. I used a piece of scrap that is 6" (152mm) wide, and it's sufficient, but if you have a wider piece, go for it. It installs in the same way as the other components, with 3" (76mm) countersunk screws.

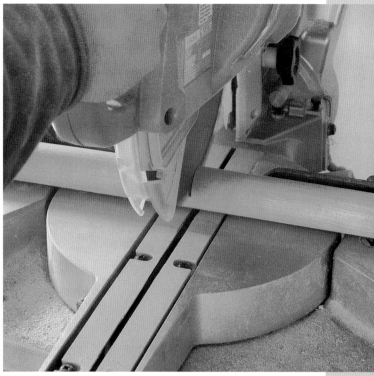

step 13 ■ Cut the hanging rod to 28½" (724mm).

step 14 ■ The hanging rod will hang from two blocks, which are made from a single 9"x6" (229mm × 152mm) scrap of ¾" (19mm) particleboard. With a 1¼" (32mm) spade bit, drill a hole in the center of the block, then rip the block in half on the table saw, or with a jigsaw or band saw. The hanging blocks screw into place. Position them so the rod is located about 10" (254mm) from the back of the armoire and about 3" (76mm) down from the top. If you want, you can install some glides to the bottom of the armoire to avoid scratching the floor.

wall
CABINET

this *cabinet is a stylish* stand-alone piece that serves as a nice intro to
building frameless cabinetry. By following the construction process and adding
your own modifications, you can take on cabinetry challenges of almost any scale.
For starters, you could add a mirror to the door to make a respectable medicine cabinet for a bathroom, or you could alter the dimensions and build a whole wall full of
kitchen cabinets.

This design presents a stripped-down cabinet — essentially just a box with
a door and a fixed shelf inside. I like the combination of a stainless-steel pull and
flat-panel door, which happens to be about the simplest option I can think of, but
the sky is the limit. You can experiment with door styles, add a molding at the top,
or match its look to the room's predominant aesthetic.

I used European-style concealed hinges because they make it easy to adjust to the
fit of the door, and they ensure that the door hangs straight. They do require a 1⅜"
(35mm) Forstner bit to drill a hole on the inside of the door (not cheap), but you'll be
amazed at how quick and easy the hinges are to install. If you don't want to use these
hinges, a surface-mounted Euro hinge (available on-line) is a good alternative.

project drawing front, side, elevation

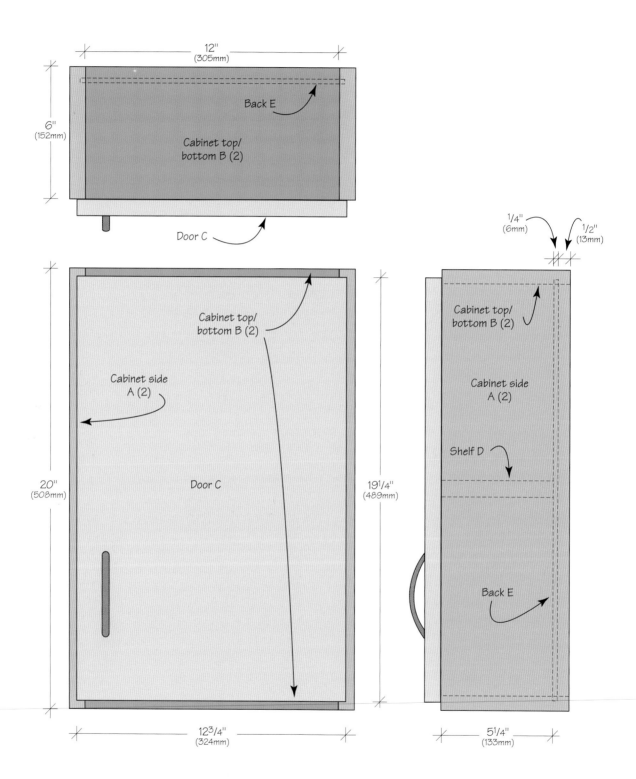

12"
(305mm)

6"
(152mm)

Back E

Cabinet top/
bottom B (2)

Door C

1/4"
(6mm)

1/2"
(13mm)

Cabinet top/
bottom B (2)

Cabinet side
A (2)

Cabinet top/
bottom B (2)

Cabinet side
A (2)

Shelf D

Door C

20"
(508mm)

19 1/4"
(489mm)

Back E

12 3/4"
(324mm)

5 1/4"
(133mm)

cutting list inches (millimeters)

REFERENCE	QUANTITY	PART	STOCK	THICKNESS	(mm)	WIDTH	(mm)	LENGTH	(mm)
A	2	cabinet sides	veneered plywood	¾	(19)	6	(152)	20	(508)
B	2	top & bottom	veneered plywood	¾	(19)	6	(152)	12	(305)
C	1	door	veneered plywood	¾	(19)	12¾	(324)	19¼	(489)
D	1	shelf	veneered plywood	¾	(19)	5¼	(133)	12	(305)
E	1	back	veneered plywood	¾	(6)	12½	(318)	19	(483)

hardware & supplies

- ■ 8 No.10 biscuits
- ■ 18' (549cm) iron-on edge-banding
- ■ 4 1¼" (6mm) screws for shelf installation
- ■ 4¾" (19mm) No.8 sheet metal screws (Phillips screw)
- ■ 1 door pull
- ■ 1 pair 35mm European-style hinges
- ■ ⅜" (10mm) overlay for a frameless cabinet) Rockler #55801
- ■ Optional, for surface-mount hinges: www.hardwaresource.com item #286138
- ■ Optional, for adjustable shelf: 4 ¼" (6mm) diameter shelf pegs Rockler #33860

step 1 ■ One of the great things about this project is that the pieces of wood required are pretty small, so you might be able to use scrap and end up with a nice cabinet for only the cost of hinges and a door pull. You'll need two sides, a top and a bottom, all cut from ¾" (19mm) plywood. If you want to, you can use solid wood for this cabinet — just make sure the grain orientation remains consistent across all parts. Because solid wood expands and contracts with seasonal changes in humidity, aligning the parts in this way prevents the wood's movement from causing problems over time. Use the dimensions in the cutting list.

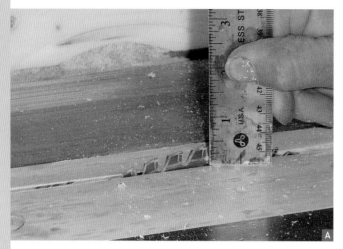

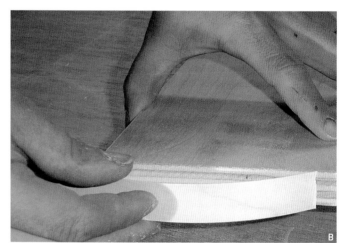

step 2 ■ The ¼" (6mm) plywood back panel is held inside a groove that runs near the back edge of the cabinet sides, top and bottom. To cut the groove, use the table saw or a router table. Set the fence ¼" (6mm) from the blade, and pass each of the four parts over it. Then move the fence to the right about ⅛" (3mm) (approximately the width of the blade), so a second pass over the blade yields a ¼"-wide (6mm) groove. Cut the groove in one of the cabinet parts, then check to make sure the material that you'll cut the back out of later will fit into the groove. If it is too tight, now is the time to make an adjustment.

step 3 ■ You've probably already noticed that the top and bottom are inset to the sides — in other words, the sides run for the entire height of the cabinet. Accordingly, you'll need to edge-band the top and bottom edges of the sides and only the front edges of the top and bottom panels. Also edge-band the front edges of the sides.

step 4 ■ The back panel is made of ¼" (6mm) veneered plywood. Cut it to size using whatever means you have at your disposal. To ensure the cabinet parts fit neatly together, dry fit them at this time. I find they go together easily if I place the structure on its side.

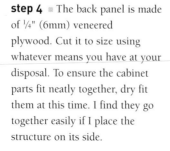

step 5 ■ While the cabinet is dry assembled, you'll want to mark for the biscuit slots. Label the corner joints so you can tell at a glance which piece is which. In the heat of the moment, with wet glue on every joint and a pile of parts in front of you, it can get a little hectic. A little planning goes a long way.

step 6 ■ Cutting the biscuits slots is straightforward. Take your time and make sure the biscuit jointer holds snugly against the workpiece and doesn't wander. Once the slots have been cut, assemble the cabinet without glue to make sure everything lines up — if there are any discrepancies, pull the cabinet apart and recut joints that don't line up. Don't consider this step optional — more than once, I've assumed my joints were perfect, only to find slight misalignments that were easily corrected as long as I hadn't yet applied the glue.

step 7 ■ Use four clamps to hold the cabinet together while the glue dries. A little bit of glue squeezed out of the corners indicates the joints have enough glue to form a strong bond — too much, though, is unnecessary and only makes for a bigger mess. In any event, I use a damp paper towel to wipe the inside and outside corners clean. Do this right away because the glue starts to set up very quickly.

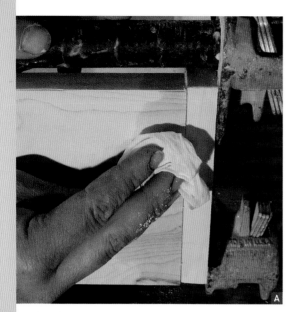

step 8 ■ While the glue is drying on the cabinet, start on the door. I designed this cabinet with a simple flat panel door made of ¾" (19mm) plywood, which is nice because it is quick and easy to make and also lends an appropriate contemporary look. Just crosscut the door blank and edge-band as usual. To lay out the hinge holes, measure in 3" (76mm) from the top and bottom edges of the door, and ¾" (19mm) in from the side. With a 1⅜" (35mm) drill bit, bore a hole for the hinge cup. Go slowly, and make sure the tip of the drill bit doesn't pop out on the other side.

TIP ■ installing hinges

Once you've installed a set or two of these hinges, you'll be a pro at it. The hinges often come in two pieces (the hinge and mounting plate). I recommend putting them together before assembly so you can understand how they work as a completed unit. It will also make their installation a more intuitive process when it comes time to attach the door to the cabinet. To begin, press the hinges into the 1⅜" (35mm) holes and screw them into place with ¾" (19mm) pan head screws.

step 9 ■ To make the shelf, rip and crosscut a piece of ¾" (19mm) plywood to dimension, and edge-band the front edge only. With the pocket-hole jig, drill two holes on the underside of each side. This shelf is fixed in place, and because it is a small shelf in a small cabinet, it will not likely be called upon to bear heavy loads, so two pocket holes on each side will provide plenty of support. If you'd like to make the shelf adjustable, drill a series of holes 1½" (38mm) apart (on center) at the front and back edges of the cabinet sides. You can then position a quartet of shelf pegs wherever you like.

step 10 ■ The shelf should fit snugly into place. Position it so you have 9" (229mm) above and below the shelf and screw it in.

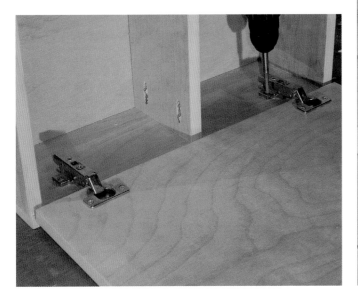

step 11 ■ To attach the door, center the door vertically on the cabinet and place a ⅛"-thick (3mm) spacer between the door and the cabinet. Secure the mounting plates with ¾" (19mm) self-tapping screws, and set the cabinet upright to see how the door hangs. By simply turning the set screws on the backs of the hinges, the door can be made to hang straight.

step 12 ■ The handle goes on by simply drilling two holes in the right spots. The exact location of the holes depends on the size of the handle and where you'd like it to go. I generally hold it in various places to see what looks right, then mark the holes and drill. Most home centers have a good selection, and I've included suppliers that I like in the back of the book.

computer
DESK

k *nockdown hardware is a mixed* bag in terms of strength and durability. The secret to success lies in knowing what to use and how to install it correctly. If you know what you're doing, you can create some burly joints that will assemble perfectly in very little time — it all comes down to making sure you lay out the fasteners correctly. I recently completed a large commercial job that included about thirty desks, and during the design phase, I experimented with different knockdown systems. In this project, I'll show you my favorite and I'll offer some tips that will make hardware installation a snap.

As with most of the projects in this book, I recommend planning out dimensions that work best for you and your space. In this case, I wanted to use no more than a full sheet of plywood, so this desk reflects that. If you don't mind spending a little more, or if you have some scraps laying around, you can increase the size pretty easily.

project drawing top, front, elevation

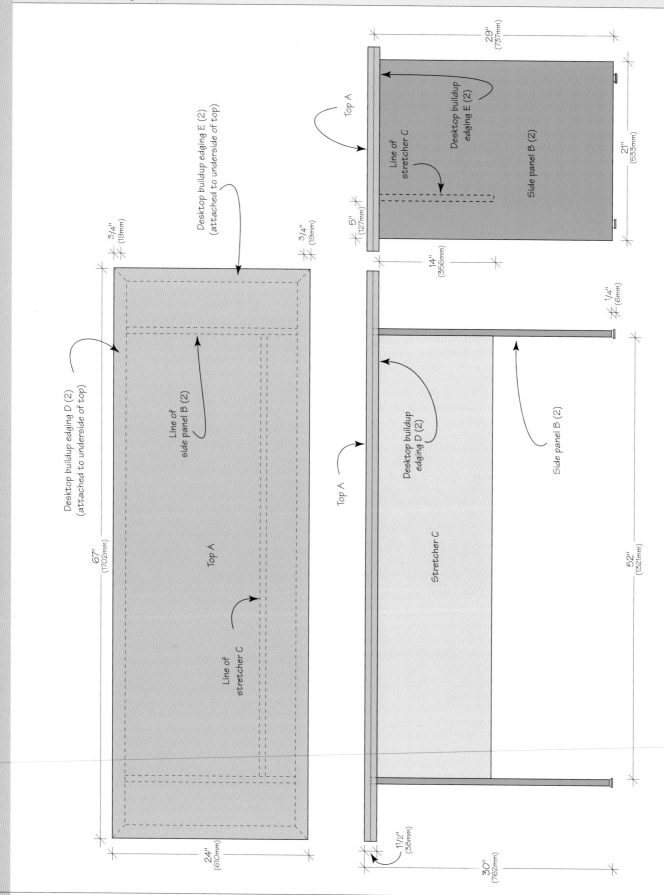

29" (737mm)

21" (533mm)

Top A

Line of stretcher C

Desktop buildup edging E (2)

Side panel B (2)

5" (127mm)

14" (356mm)

Desktop buildup edging E (2) (attached to underside of top)

Desktop buildup edging D (2) (attached to underside of top)

3/4" (19mm)

3/4" (19mm)

Line of side panel B (2)

Top A

Line of stretcher C

67" (1702mm)

24" (610mm)

Top A

Desktop buildup edging D (2)

Side panel B (2)

1/4" (6mm)

Stretcher C

52" (1321mm)

11/2" (38mm)

30" (762mm)

cutting list inches [millimeters]

REFERENCE	QUANTITY	PART	STOCK	THICKNESS	(mm)	WIDTH	(mm)	LENGTH	(mm)
A	1	top	veneered plywood	¾	(19)	24	(610)	66	(1676)
B	2	side panels	veneered plywood	¾	(19)	21	(533)	29	(737)
C	1	stretcher	veneered plywood	¾	(19)	14	(356)	52	(1321)
D	2	desktop buildup edging	veneered plywood	¾	(19)	1½	(38)	67	(1702)
E	2	desktop buildup edging	veneered plywood	¾	(19)	1½	(38)	24	(610)

hardware & supplies

■ 4 1"-long (25mm) "L" brackets

■ 4 fastener sets (4 bolts, 4 cross-dowels)

■ 1 set of 4 leveling feet

■ 40-50 1¼" (32mm) screws

step 1 ■ Start by ripping the plywood down the middle at 24" (610mm).

step 2 ■ Crosscut one of the two halves to 67" (1702mm) to make the top. This leaves you with a 29"-long (737mm) offcut. Crosscutting veneered plywood is tricky, so if you're getting any tearout on the bottom side of the cut, firmly place masking tape along the area where the cut will be made. This keeps the fibers of the veneer in place instead of blowing out at random when the blade passes through.

step 3 ■ With the fence moved to 21" (533mm), I rerip the second half of the sheet of plywood and also the offcut from the first half of the sheet. This rip cut will turn the offcut into a 29"×21" (737mm × 533mm) panel, which is the right dimension for a side panel (I chose the length of the top so you could get both the top and the side panel by only having to make one crosscut).

step 4 ■ Now you can crosscut the 96"×21" (2438mm × 533mm) piece to 29" (737mm) to produce the second side panel.

step 5 ■ At this point, you should have a couple of scraps that measure approximately 67"× 21" (1702mm × 533mm), and 96"× 3" (2438mm × 76mm). Crosscut the 67"× 21" (1702mm × 533mm) piece at 59" (1499mm), then rip to 14" (356mm) to form the horizontal stretcher that will join the two side panels.

step 6 ■ Rip the 96"× 3" (2438mm × 76mm) scrap down the middle and it will provide you with enough material to double up the edge on the underside of the top. This will proved a stiffer surface, especially along the front edge, and also adds a visual layer that bulks up the desk top.

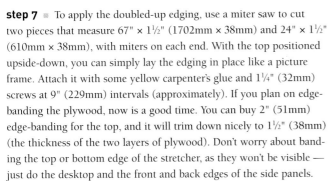

step 7 ◾ To apply the doubled-up edging, use a miter saw to cut two pieces that measure 67" × 1½" (1702mm × 38mm) and 24" × 1½" (610mm × 38mm), with miters on each end. With the top positioned upside-down, you can simply lay the edging in place like a picture frame. Attach it with some yellow carpenter's glue and 1¼" (32mm) screws at 9" (229mm) intervals (approximately). If you plan on edge-banding the plywood, now is a good time. You can buy 2" (51mm) edge-banding for the top, and it will trim down nicely to 1½" (38mm) (the thickness of the two layers of plywood). Don't worry about banding the top or bottom edge of the stretcher, as they won't be visible — just do the desktop and the front and back edges of the side panels.

step 8 ◾ It might seem premature, but now is a good time to attach the leveling feet to the side panels. It is easier than trying to do it later when the desk is fully assembled. The feet will come with directions for their installation — it is generally a matter of drilling holes, ⅜" (10mm) in most cases into the bottom edge of the panel and driving in the threaded plastic sleeves with a hammer. The metal feet then screw in easily.

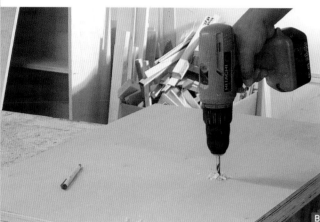

step 9 ■ The knockdown hardware set I like to use for this application consists of two parts: a long bolt and a cross dowel. You'll use two sets on each end of the stretcher/side panel joint (a total of four bolts and four cross dowels). Begin by drilling two holes on each side panel for the bolts. The first hole is located 6" (152mm) in from the back edge of the panel, and 1½" (38mm) down from the top. The second hole is located 6" (152mm) in from the back edge, and 12½" (318mm) down from the top. The bolt diameter is ¼" (6mm), so drill a hole ⅜" (10mm) wide. This will allow for wiggle room without creating a sloppy joint. Once you've drilled the holes in one side panel, you can place it on top of the second panel and use it as a template for drilling the second set of holes.

step 10 ■ You'll have to drill holes into both of the stretcher's ends. These holes correspond exactly to the holes in the side panels, so they are located 1½" (38mm) and 12½" (318mm) down from the top of the stretcher, respectively. The holes can be ⅜" (10mm) in diameter, and they need to be 3" (76mm) deep. Drill them slowly and carefully to ensure that you bore them parallel to the length of the stretcher. If they wander too much toward one side or the other, the drill bit will burst through the veneer in the wrong spot, and there is no fix for this mistake (unfortunately, this is the voice of experience speaking).

step 11 ■ The final holes in the stretcher are drilled on its face, and they intersect the 3" (76mm) deep holes that go in from the edge. They need to be ½" (13mm) in diameter (use a Forstner or spade bit for best results, and make sure the back side of the stretcher is firmly placed against scrap wood to prevent tearout). The first of these holes is located 1½" (38mm) down from the top and 2½" (64mm) from the edge of the stretcher. The second is located 12½" (318mm) down from the top, and 2½" (64mm) from the edge. You'll have to drill these holes on both ends of the stretcher.

step 12 ■ Prior to finishing, assemble the desk to make sure everything lines up properly. If you have trouble getting the bolt to thread into the cross dowel, you can slightly widen the ⅜" (10mm) hole in the end of the stretcher by redrilling the holes and wiggling the drill bit around a little bit this time. Work slowly so you don't overdo it. This method should buy you enough space to align the hardware as needed.

step 13 ■ When the glue between the desktop and the edging has dried, you can sand them flush. This job goes very quickly with a belt sander fitted with a 60-grit belt. I softened the hard edge with a random-orbit sander.

step 14 ■ The desktop is attached to the base with small angle brackets. The overhang of the desktop and the built-up edging keep them pretty well hidden. Although it may be tempting, do not finish the entire desk while it is assembled. The finish will most likely glue the stretcher to the side panels, and you'll be in for a real battle when you try to pull the desk apart.

waste
BASKET

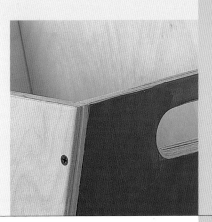

here's a simple design that adds style to any home office or other room. Initially I considered building this wastebasket in such a way that it tapered outward on all four sides instead of two, but doing so requires complicated (compound) angles, which are a lot of work that doesn't contribute that much more to the design. Tapering one pair of sides and keeping the other pair perpendicular to the floor lends enough interest to the piece, while keeping the construction techniques fairly simple. It also allows the wastebasket to fit flush against a wall.

The piece goes together with glued and screwed butt joints. The screws are countersunk. I used shiny zinc screws and did not plug them because I like the contrast that they provide to the wood. Also, the ½" (13mm) plywood is a bit too thin for me to comfortably drill into. Thicker materials, in my view, are much better suited to counterbored and plugged holes.

I also cut handholds into the wastebasket's sides, which I think provide an attractive minimalist detail. You can also use something that screws on, depending on the look you're going for. Like most pieces in this book, this wastebasket could be finished in any number of ways. In this case, I chose a combination of natural birch and paint.

project drawing top, front, elevation

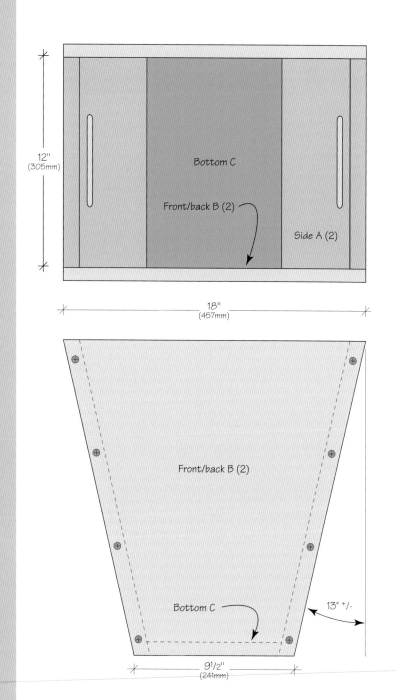

12"
(305mm)

Bottom C

Front/back B (2)

Side A (2)

18"
(457mm)

Front/back B (2)

Bottom C

13° +/-

9½"
(241mm)

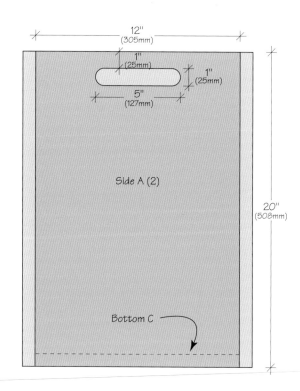

12"
(305mm)

1"
(25mm)

1"
(25mm)

5"
(127mm)

Side A (2)

20"
(508mm)

Bottom C

cutting list inches [millimeters]

hardware & supplies

■ 16 1¼" (32mm) screws

REFERENCE	QUANTITY	PART	STOCK	THICKNESS	(mm)	WIDTH	(mm)	LENGTH	(mm)
A	2	sides	veneered plywood	½	[13]	12	[305]	20	[508]
B	2	front & back	veneered plywood	½	[13]	18	[457]	18	[457]
C	1	bottom	veneered plywood	¾	[19]	10	[254]	12	[305]

step 1 ■ This project requires only five parts: a pair of straight sides, a pair of tapered sides and a bottom. The straight sides are simple rectangles that measure 20" × 12" (508mm × 305mm). Start by cutting them to size with whatever technology you have at your command.

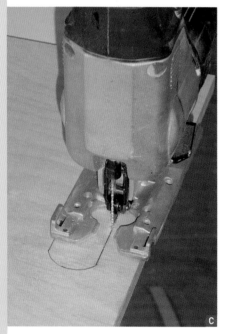

step 2 ■ To cut handholds into the straight sides, simply draw a shape onto one side and cut it with a jigsaw, then clean the cut with sanding drums as needed. I cut a handle which consists of a rectangle with a radius on each end — a rectangular-shaped handle would've been quicker and easier, but I like the look of the radius.

To get the jigsaw started, I drilled a ⅜" (10mm) hole in the middle of the handhold, but if you fancy yourself a hotshot with a jigsaw, you can do a plunge cut here.

Once the handhold cutout on one of the straight sides has been sanded (but before it has been routed), you can use it as a pattern for the handhold on the second straight side. I simply place the straight sides on top of each other and trace the cutout, then cut and sand the second handhold. A roundover bit in a handheld router will soften the edges, making them easy on the hands.

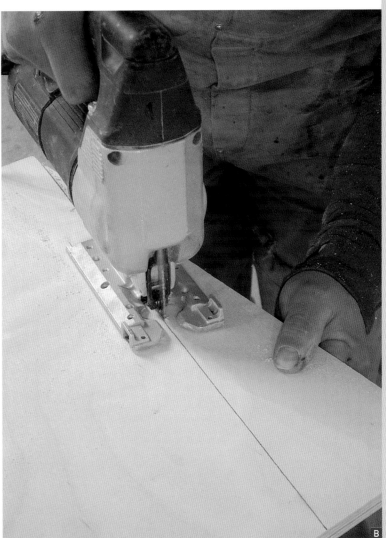

step 3 ■ The tapered sides begin as squares that measure 18" × 18" (457mm × 457mm). To lay out the taper, measure in 4¼" (108mm) from each side on the bottom edge. Using a straightedge, draw a line from each top corner to the mark on the corresponding side of the rectangle. With a jigsaw or band saw, cut the tapers.

step 4 ■ Sand the freshly cut edges with whatever means you have at your disposal. Belt sanders are nice because they do the job quickly, but very coarse (36- or 60-grit) paper used with a hand sander is a perfectly reasonable substitute.

step 5 ■ With a countersink bit, drill a series of holes up the edge of the tapered sides. Doing this prior to assembly makes the process go a little easier.

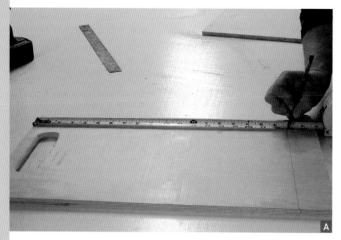

step 6 ■ Before assembly, trim the straight sides to length using an angled cut along their bottom edge. You can use a circular saw, jigsaw, band saw or table saw to make this cut. For a jigsaw (my saw of choice), adjust the base to a 13° angle, then lay out a line that is 18½" (470mm) from the top of the side. Make the cut and sand flush any rough edges.

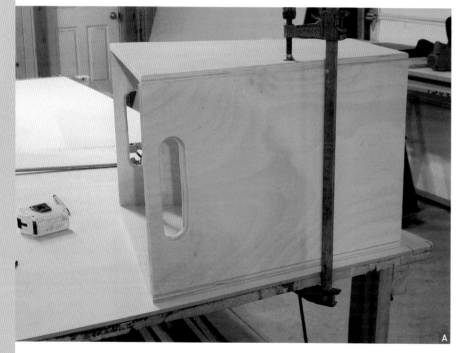

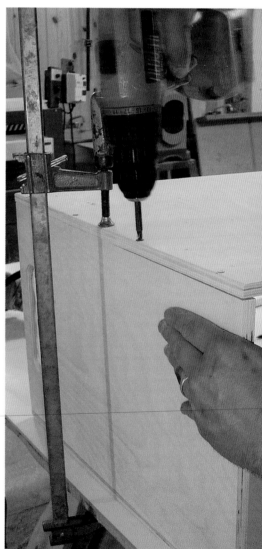

step 7 ■ To assemble the wastebasket, lay one of the tapered sides flat on the bench and position a straight side perpendicular to it (sticking up in the air). A thin bead of wood glue helps reinforce this joint. Then place the other tapered side on top of the straight side and clamp it into place. The whole thing should look like the letter C when viewed straight ahead. If the joint between the tapered side on the bottom and the vertically positioned straight side wiggles out of alignment, don't sweat it — you'll be able to readjust it in a minute. For now, make sure the edges line up between the top tapered side and the straight side — loosen and tighten the clamp as needed to ease it into place. Secure this joint with screws installed through the countersunk holes, then flip the assembly upside down and secure the opposing joint. The hard part is over, so wipe up any glue that squeezes out and install the final side.

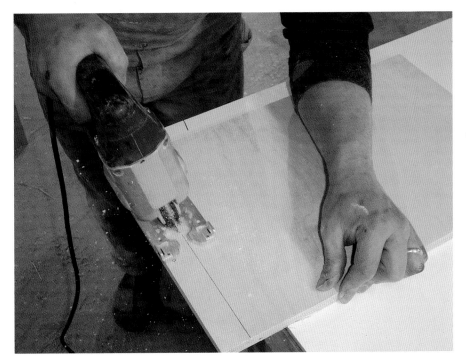

step 8 ■ The bottom starts as a rectangle that is 12" × 10" (305mm × 254mm). All you have to do is cut an angle on each of its long sides so it can be pressed into the wastebasket and will fit snugly. You can use a table saw with a miter gauge and angle the blade to 13° , or you can use a jigsaw or circular saw with the base tilted to 13°. A band saw with its table angled would work fine too. After the cut is made, the bottom will measure 12" × 9" (305mm × 229mm).

step 9 ■ The bottom, as I indicated, presses in from the top. You can give it a tap with a nonmarring hammer or a piece of soft scrap wood to make sure it is snug. Because it wedges into place, you don't need mechanical fasteners on the bottom; just glue it in.

step 10 ■ The edges of the wastebasket benefit from a light sanding with a hand sander. When you're done, the parts will appear to flow together.

clothes
HAMPER

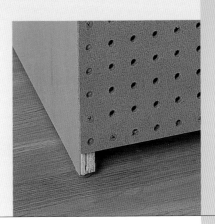

i *had a few goals in mind when* I designed this hamper. In addition to looking cool, I wanted it to be reasonably lightweight so it would be easy to carry around even when filled, and I wanted it to be made of a material that allows air to circulate so odors are kept to a minimum. The solution to both issues came in a humble form: good, old pegboard. For structural stability, I used ³⁄₄"-thick (19mm) plywood for the sides (a beefy surface to fasten the handles onto). But the visual impact of the piece, as well as much of its practicality, comes from the uniqueness of the pegboard.

Pegboard is available in different grades. I like the darker color of the tempered pegboard, which also has a nice sheen that doesn't require an additional finish. My local home center stocked some curved brushed nickel handles at a surprisingly good price, and their dramatic shape inspired me to cut a curve across the top of the lid as well. And, though I didn't try this at home, it would be nifty and useful to mount the hamper on a set of inexpensive casters.

project drawing top, front, elevation

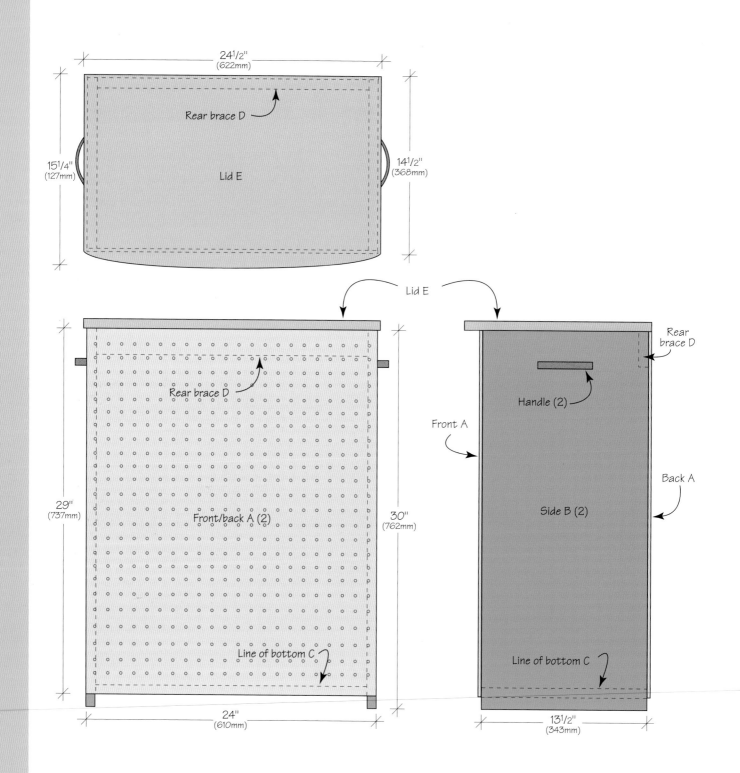

24¹/2"
(622mm)

Rear brace D

15¹/4"
(127mm)

Lid E

14¹/2"
(368mm)

Lid E

Rear brace D

Handle (2)

Rear brace D

29"
(737mm)

Front/back A (2)

30"
(762mm)

Front A

Side B (2)

Back A

Line of bottom C

Line of bottom C

24"
(610mm)

13¹/2"
(343mm)

cutting list inches (millimeters)

REFERENCE	QUANTITY	PART	STOCK	THICKNESS	(mm)	WIDTH	(mm)	LENGTH	(mm)
A	2	front & back	pegboard	¼	(6)	24	(610)	29	(737)
B	2	sides	veneered plywood	¾	(19)	13½	(343)	30	(762)
C	1	bottom	veneered plywood	¾	(19)	13½	(343)	22½	(572)
D	1	top	veneered plywood	¾	(19)	16	(406)	26	(660)
E	1	rear brace	veneered plywood	¾	(19)	2	(51)	22½	(572)
F	1	lid	veneered plywood	¾	(19)	15¼	(387)	24½	(622)

hardware & supplies

- 1 pair 2½" (64mm) butt hinges
- 2 cabinet door pulls
- 1 set of 4 rubber bumpers
- 16 1¼" (32mm) pockethole screws

step 1 ■ Like most projects, this one begins with cutting the parts to size. The pegboard is sold in 48" × 24" (1219mm × 610mm) pieces, which are easy to work with. You'll also need a pair of side panels and a bottom panel.

step 2 ■ The side panels will fasten to the bottom panel with pocket-hole screws and glue. Cut the pocket holes on the underside of the bottom panel so they're not exposed on the inside of the hamper. You could also use biscuits here.

step 3 ■ Set the bottom panel 1" (25mm) from the floor. I measured up 1" (25mm) on the side panels and drew a line so I could see where to place the bottom panel. You can now assemble the sides and bottom so they resemble a U shape when viewed from the front. A clamp holds the panels in position and keeps them from slipping out of alignment.

step 4 ■ This is a convenient time to attach the rubber feet. You could do it later, but I do it here because I know that I'll be moving the hamper around during assembly, and I don't want to risk damaging it.

step 5 ■ If you'll want to paint or stain the sides, do it now. You won't have to worry about masking off the edges of the pegboard to keep the paint off, and the job will go more quickly.

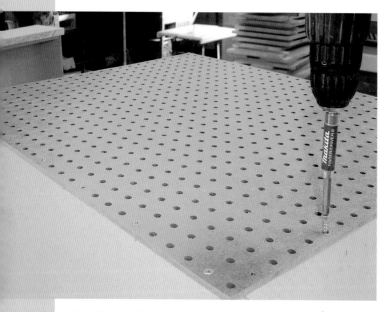

step 6 ■ Just before screwing on the front and back panels, run a very thin bead of glue along the edge of the sides — not so much that it will slop out but enough to provide extra strength once it has set up. You can place the screws right through the holes in the pegboard [I suggest skipping about 3" (76mm) between screws]. I used galvanized drywall screws because I like the galvanized finish and because their heads are big enough to securely tighten without pressing through the holes in the pegboard.

step 7 ■ The hinges that attach the lid must screw into something solid, so I made a simple brace from scrap plywood. It measures 2" (51mm) wide and ¾" (19mm) thick, which is beefy enough to support the lid.

step 8 ▪ The brace should fit snugly, and is a snap to install. Attach it to the hamper sides with pocket-hole screws.

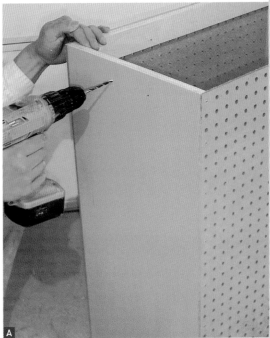

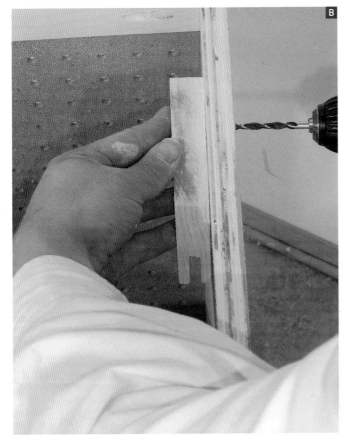

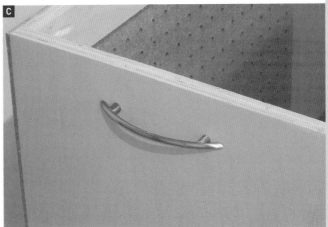

step 9 ▪ To attach the handles, you'll need to know how far apart to drill the screw holes. Measure from the center of one hole to the center of the other — in my case, the distance is 3¾" (95mm). Measure down 1½" (38mm) from the top of the hamper's side, and 7" (178mm) from the edge, and make a light, almost invisible mark. This is the center of the panel (it measures 14" (356mm) with the pegboard front and back attached). By dividing the measurement of the handle's holes in half, you'll know how far to measure to the right and to the left of the center mark. In my case, I divide 3¾" (95mm) by 2, and get 1⅞" (47mm). Therefore, I measure 1⅞" (47mm) from the left of the center mark, and 1⅞" (47mm) from the right side, and doing so provides the right spacing for the handle holes. Just make sure each of these holes are located 1½" (38mm) from the top. Then drill the holes. Place a block of scrap wood on the back side of the hole to prevent tearout as the drill bit emerges through the panel. Make sure you don't drill into your hand — I mention this because, even though it sounds dumb, I have actually done it before.

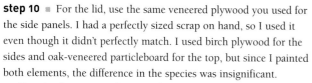

step 10 ■ For the lid, use the same veneered plywood you used for the side panels. I had a perfectly sized scrap on hand, so I used it even though it didn't perfectly match. I used birch plywood for the sides and oak-veneered particleboard for the top, but since I painted both elements, the difference in the species was insignificant.

For visual interest and to complement the shape of the handles, I drew and cut a curve across the front edge of the lid. Laying out curves can be a complicated affair, but I used the simplest method I know, which is to draw the curve freehand on one half of the piece. With a jigsaw, carefully cut it out, then trace the cutout on the other half. A couple of minutes of sanding will produce a smooth, eye-pleasing curve.

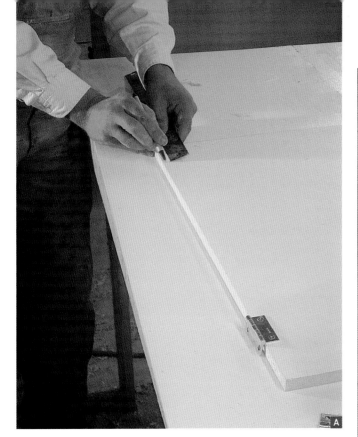

step 11 ■ With the lid upside down, the butt hinges simply screw in along the back edge. Place them about 2½" (64mm) in from the sides (the exact distance isn't critical). Align the hinges so the barrel is positioned just past the edge of the lid.

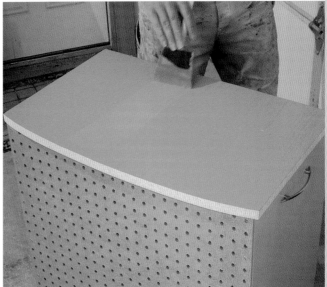

step 12 ■ To attach the lid to the hamper, position the lid behind the hamper as if it were fully open. With one hinge on the edge of the brace, get one screw fastened fairly tightly — the first one is the hard one. Once you have one screw in place, you can take your time evening up the other hinge and screwing it down. When the second hinge has been screwed down, you can go back and drive the final screw into the first hinge.

step 13 ■ For the final step, finish the top with your choice of paint, stain or varnish.

tv
STAND

basically a cabinet that sits on a base, the TV stand is similar to the blanket chest but it presents some neat variations in the way the base goes together and also in the configuration of the storage area.

The dimensions used in this project reflect the dimensions of my own modest entertainment needs. Before building your own version, do some measuring and sketching to determine the size and proportions that will work best for you. The basic concept can be adapted to any set of dimensions you need. You can also easily divide the cabinet interior with shelves, partitions or drawers. Or make a really large cabinet that the TV will fit inside. You might even want to add doors.

You can use any of a variety of simple ways to join the cabinet panels: pocket screws, through screws, biscuits and splines all come to mind. I left the back mostly open, to allow easy access to the various cables and components involved, but I also wanted plenty of strength to prevent the cabinet from slouching (racking) from side-to-side. As a solution, I decided to reinforce the cabinet at the sides with two ¾"-thick (19mm) supports, which I glued and screwed into place. This result is the best of all worlds: a rock-solid cabinet and plenty of clearance where you need it.

project drawing front, side, elevation

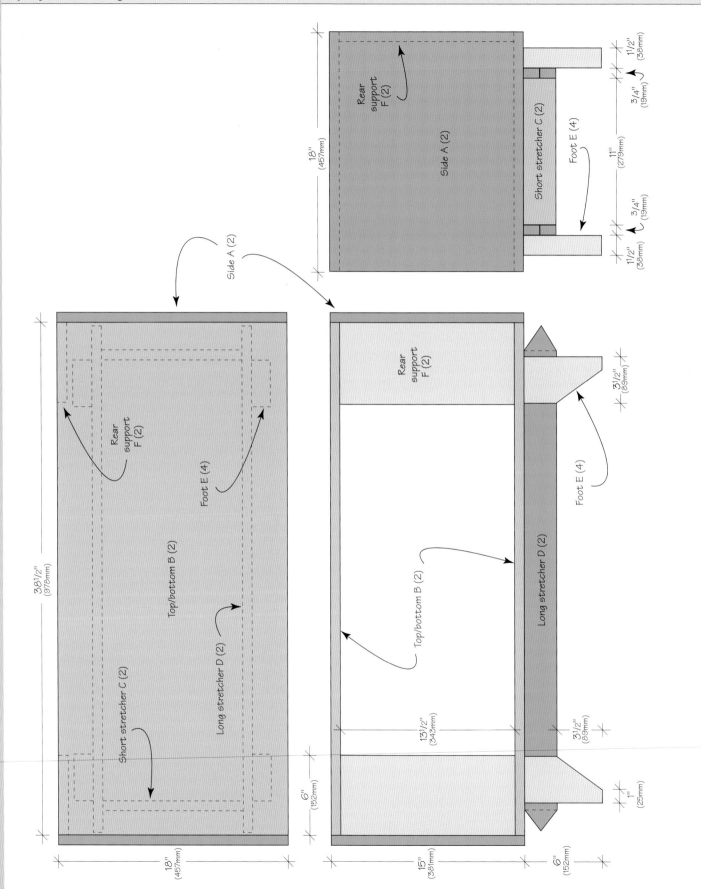

cutting list inches (millimeters)

REFERENCE	QUANTITY	PART	STOCK	THICKNESS	(mm)	WIDTH	(mm)	LENGTH	(mm)	COMMENTS
A	2	sides	veneered plywood	¾	(19)	18	(457)	38½	(978)	
B	2	top & bottom	veneered plywood	¾	(19)	18	(457)	15	(381)	
C	2	short stretchers	veneered plywood	¾	(19)	2½	(64)	11	(279)	solid wood can also be used
D	2	long stretchers	veneered plywood	¾	(19)	2½	(64)	38	(965)	solid wood can also be used
E	4	feet	2x4	1½	(38)	3½	(89)	6	(152)	
F	2	rear supports	veneered ply	¾	(19)	6	(152)	13½	(343)	

hardware & supplies

- 30-40 1¼" (32mm) pockethole screws

- 15-20 1¼" (32mm) drywall screws

step 1 ■ Although you could start by building the cabinet, I jumped in and made the base first. You could use solid wood for the stretchers that compose the base, but I used ¾"-thick (19mm) veneered plywood, a perfectly reasonable choice as well. Either way, begin by ripping the stretchers to width and crosscutting them to length.

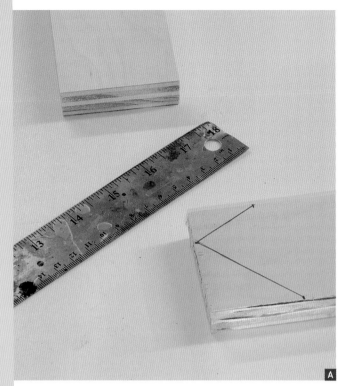

A

B

step 2 ∎ I made an asymmetrical profile cut on each end of the long stretchers. If you want to save time, you can omit this detail, but if you don't mind spending a few minutes, it adds considerably to the visual interest of the base. The profile consists of a straight cut at the upper and lower edges of the stretcher. To lay out for the lower cut, measure in 1¾" (45mm) from the bottom and from the edge, and draw a diagonal line (it will be at a 45° angle). To lay out the upper line, measure in 1¼" (32mm) from the edge and connect this point to the tip that is ¾" (19mm) from the top edge of the stretcher. Use a jigsaw to cut out the profile. You can clean up any irregularities with a handheld sander. Then use the finished piece to trace a pattern onto the remaining ends of the stretchers.

step 3 ▪ On the inside ends of the short stretchers, cut the pocket holes which will allow you to join the stretchers.

A

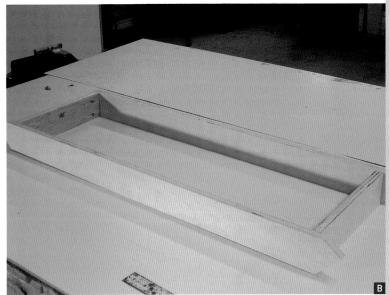

B

step 4 ▪ You can now glue and screw the short stretchers onto the inside face of the long stretchers. If you haven't used pocket screws in the past, you may want to clamp the pieces together to make sure nothing wiggles out of alignment. Because I've done this a lot, I find that I can keep the parts in place by working on one joint at a time and positioning the assembly so gravity holds things where I need them.

step 5 ■ For the feet, cut four pieces of 2×4 that are each 6" (152mm) long, then lay out for the angled cut that helps to visually lighten them up: measure 3½" (89mm) up on one side, and 2½" (64mm) across the bottom from that side. By drawing a line between these two points and cutting with a jigsaw, you'll have the first foot ready to use as a pattern for the other three.

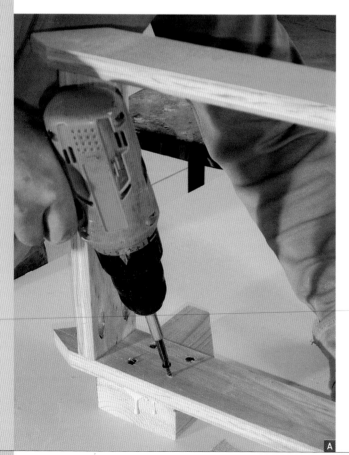

step 6 ■ Glue and screw the feet onto the outside face of the stretchers. The change of thickness across the front of the base makes it interesting.

step 7 ▪ The cabinet itself is quick and easy to put together. You'll need two sides and two identical panels for the top and bottom. Drill a row of pocket holes along the underside of the shorter edges of the top and bottom panels.

step 8 ▪ Work on getting one row of pocket holes secured at a time. Trying to clamp all the parts together can be frustrating, so I avoid it entirely. Either place the top panel upright so that you are screwing downward toward the bench, or position the panels on their edges and clamp across them for stability.

step 9 ▪ Drill pocket holes on three sides of the back supports.

step 10 ▪ Install the back supports with glue and plenty of screws. Televisions are heavy, and I'd rather err on the side of overdoing it when it comes to reinforcing the cabinet. Attach the finished cabinet to the base by screwing it down through the top side of the bottom panel and into the base. Or run stretchers across the top of the base, as shown in the Blanket Chest project.

media storage RACK

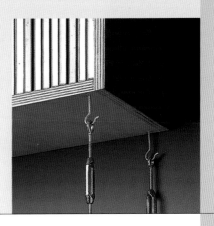

CDs and DVDs *pile up* pretty quickly around my place, and I'm pretty sure I'm not alone. Here's a smart, simple storage unit that comes together in very little time — an hour or so. This project provides specific instructions for an 18" × 30" (457mm × 762mm) rack, but you may decide to alter the dimensions depending on how much stuff you need to store. Twenty-eight CDs fit into a 12" (305mm) space, so count them up and plan accordingly. This two-tiered 30" (762mm) rack holds up to 170 CDs — I use the negative space in the middle to display knickknacks, but you can fill it with CDs and gain even more storage capacity.

In terms of the construction, I had some scrap ¾"-thick (19mm) plywood, which worked out great. You could reasonably substitute medium-density overlay (MDO), medium-density fiberboard (MDF), or even solid wood, depending on your preference and your budget. For the joinery, I used countersunk through screws, but you can utilize pocket screws, biscuits, dowels or nails instead. If you want to practice more advanced joinery methods, I would suggest a dado and rabbet joint or finger joints.

project drawing top, front, elevation

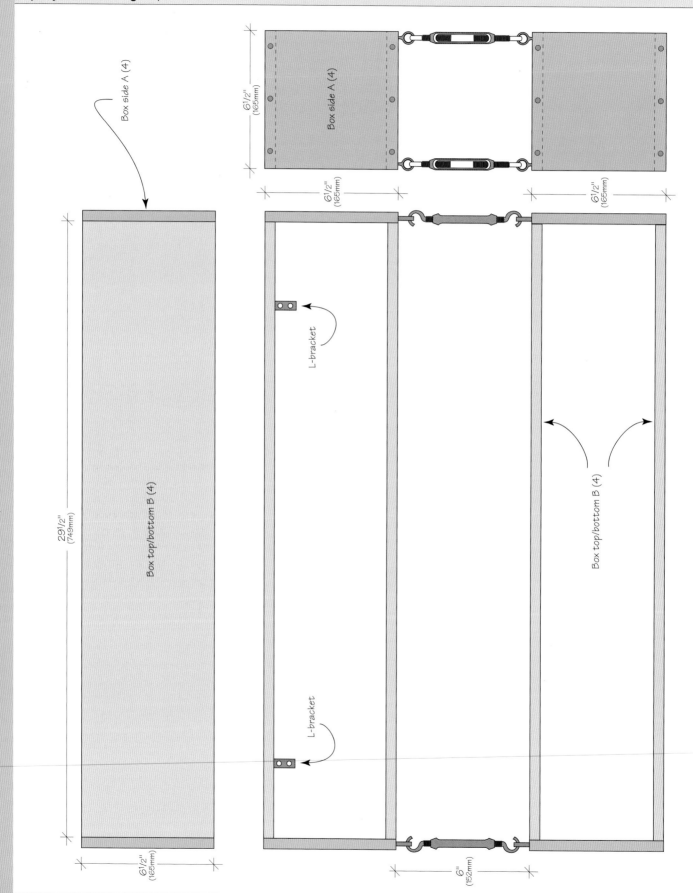

Box side A (4)

Box side A (4)

6¹⁄₂"
(165mm)

6¹⁄₂"
(165mm)

6¹⁄₂"
(165mm)

L-bracket

29¹⁄₂"
(749mm)

Box top/bottom B (4)

Box top/bottom B (4)

L-bracket

6¹⁄₂"
(165mm)

6"
(152mm)

cutting list inches [millimeters]

REFERENCE	QUANTITY	PART	STOCK	THICKNESS	(mm)	WIDTH	(mm)	LENGTH	(mm)
A	4	box sides	birch veneer plywood	¾	[19]	6½	[165]	6½	[165]
B	4	box tops & bottoms	birch veneer plywood	¾	[19]	6½	[165]	29½	[749]

hardware & supplies

- 4 eye screws
- 4 screw-in hooks
- 4 4" (152mm) turnbuckles
- 2 2½"- (64mm) long L-brackets

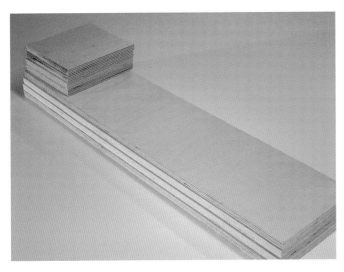

step 1 ■ The storage rack is comprised principally of two four-sided boxes that are held together by turnbuckles and eye screws. Cut out the parts for the boxes. You'll need four sides, four tops and bottoms.

step 2 ■ I used countersunk screws to assemble the rack. Put a countersinking bit into your drill and drill a series of holes along the top and bottom edges of the sides. Three screws per edge provides plenty of strength.

step 3 ■ I used a water-based stain to color the sides of the boxes. It's relatively simple to apply prior to assembly. Stain the sides after drilling the countersunk holes for the screw heads — this way, the stain will cover up any tear-out that may occur.

step 4 ■ With a clamp at the ready, lay out a thin bead of glue and put the boxes together one joint at a time. Use a wet paper towel or rag to wipe up any glue that squeezes out.

step 5 ■ To ensure that the parts are flush along the front edge, use a sander and 80-grit paper. This is also a good way to clean up any stain that may have dripped onto the edges during step 3.

step 6 ■ The upper box gets fastened to the wall with *L* brackets. The brackets are screwed onto the underside of the box's top. My trick here is to put the brackets in place and mark where the rear screw will go in. Then spin the bracket out of the way and drive the screw in tightly with the drill. With some effort, you should be able to spin the bracket back into place so it sits flush against the wall. Then insert the other screw in the bracket.

step 7 ▪ Drill a hole into each of the four corners of the top side of the lower box and also into the four corners of the bottom side of the upper box.

step 8 ▪ The eye screws are too hard to turn by hand, but with a long bolt or something similar, you can twist them in easily. The lower box gets the four eye screws, and the upper box gets the hooks. To screw in the hooks, use a pair of needle-nose pliers.

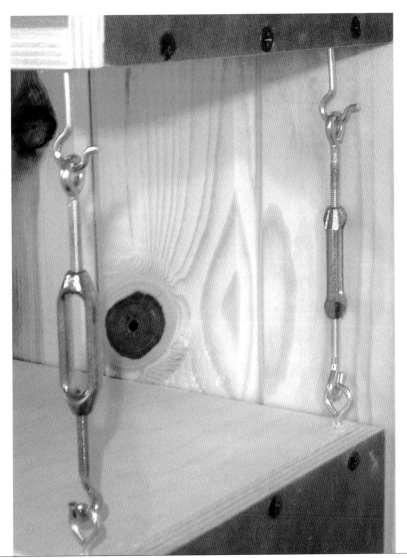

step 9 ▪ To install the unit, simply screw the upper box into the wall (be sure to either hit studs with your screws or use an appropriate anchor of your choice). Once the upper box is in place, hang the turnbuckles from the hooks and suspend the lower box from the turnbuckles. The inherent adjustability of the turnbuckles allows you to level out the lower box.

danish modern
COFFEE TABLE

though *I appreciate many historical* styles, Danish Modern furniture is probably my favorite. Like many genre labels, this one encompasses such a diverse range of forms that it has become watered down. At its essence, however, I see several exciting commonalities: sleek lines; rich, dark finishes; and quiet details that make me wish I had come up with them. Although this coffee table does not draw heavily from a particular Danish Modern designer, I think that it is a fitting tribute to the style as a whole.

The table is principally comprised of a flat top, a box attached to its underside to create a shelf, and four 16" (406mm) screw-on wooden legs. Some people might consider using pre-made table legs like these cheating, but I am all for using them. With enough time and tooling, you could certainly fabricate your own, but when time and resources are limited, you need to pick your battles.

I found these round, tapered legs at a local home center and saw possibilities for all kinds of contemporary pieces. They also come in 28" (711mm) lengths, so you may consider using them for taller tables as well. The ones I found are made of ash, which is one of my favorite light-colored hardwoods, but for this piece, I prefer a darker finish, so I applied a walnut-toned stain.

One of the details that I love about this piece is the bevel on the edge of the tabletop — it is a subtle element that lends a slightly more sophisticated feel to the piece. The angle of the bevel is important, as well: too much and it feels too extreme; too little, and it may not have enough impact. I suggest a happy medium somewhere in the neighborhood of 20° to 25°. If you want to simplify the design to save time, you can eliminate the bevel altogether.

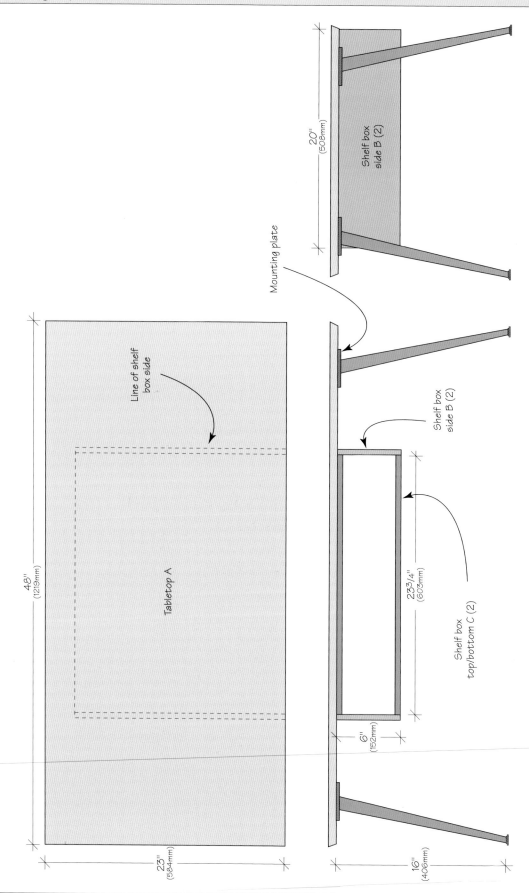

20"
(508mm)

Shelf box
side B (2)

Mounting plate

Line of shelf
box side

Tabletop A

48"
(1219mm)

Shelf box
side B (2)

23³/₄"
(603mm)

Shelf box
top/bottom C (2)

6"
(152mm)

23"
(584mm)

16"
(406mm)

cutting list inches (millimeters)

REFERENCE	QUANTITY	PART	STOCK	THICKNESS	(mm)	WIDTH	(mm)	LENGTH	(mm)
A	1	tabletop	maple veneer plywood	¾	(19)	23	(584)	48	(1219)
B	2	shelf-box sides	maple veneer plywood	¾	(19)	6	(152)	20	(508)
C	2	shelf-box top & bottom	maple veneer plywood	¾	(19)	20	(508)	23¾	(603)

hardware & supplies

- 4 16"-long (406mm) turned legs
- 4 angled mounting plates
- 25' (7.6m) iron-on maple edge-banding
- 20 1¼" (32mm) drywall screws
- 16 ⅝" (16mm) panhead sheet metal screws

step 1 ■ The logical place to start is with the top. Although you could use solid wood, a fine veneered plywood simplifies and speeds up the construction immensely. Begin by cutting a 48" × 22" (1219mm × 559mm) top. Use a table saw or a straight-edge and a circular saw or jigsaw.

step 2 ■ To crosscut large pieces of plywood, I prefer to use a straightedge and a jigsaw. To correctly position the straightedge, first determine the offset between the edge of the blade and the edge of the jigsaw (or circular saw) base plate. Once you've measured it, you can add that number to the length you're cutting out. In this case, the top will measure 48" (1219mm), and the offset is ¹⁵⁄₁₆" (24mm), so I positioned my straightedge at 49⁵⁄₁₆" (1253mm) from the edge of the plywood.

step 3 ■ To cut the bevel on the edge of the plywood top, angle the jigsaw base to 25°. In my experience, using a straightedge for this operation doesn't usually work — the blade wanders and cuts an eccentric angle — so I find it easiest to make the cut freehand. In this case, use the edge of the plywood as a visual guide. If you go slowly enough, you can cut just about anything freehand. Practice on some scrap if you need to build confidence. Position your body directly behind the saw (rather than beside it) and look directly down at the blade. Good body position enables you to see exactly where you're cutting and to make the cut as even as possible.

step 4 ■ Even the best freehand cuts usually need a little help. I use a random-orbit sander with 80-grit paper to even out any irregularities. A belt sander also works but tends to take off a lot of material at once, so be forewarned.

step 5 ■ Iron-on edge-banding is truly plywood's best friend. An ordinary household iron set at the highest temperature does the job quickly and easily (see the "Edge-Banding 101" sidebar later in this chapter.)

step 6 ■ I use scissors to clip the ends flush. The trick to producing a cut that requires no sanding is to press the flat inside edge of the scissors blade against the plywood.

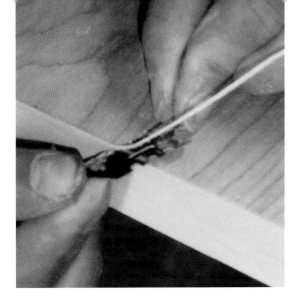

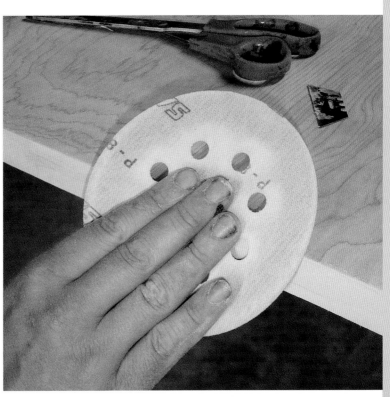

step 7 ■ A utility knife trims away the parts of the edge-banding that protrude above the plywood. Hold the back edge of the blade about ⅛" (3mm) to ³⁄₁₆" (5mm) up in the air. Doing so keeps the blade at an angle that allows it to cut very smoothly.

step 8 ■ With just a bit of sanding with 120- or 150-grit paper, the edge-banding is blended in so well it looks like it has always been there.

step 9 ■ Cut the four parts for the shelf-box (two sides, a top and a bottom). You can assemble the box using any of several methods including biscuits, plugged screws, finish nails or screws that are countersunk but otherwise left exposed. I've chosen countersunk screws. With a countersinking bit, drill a row of holes along both the top and bottom edges of both side panels.

step 10 ■ Assembling furniture is very often a straightforward process, but it helps to consider the order in which you perform the various steps. In this case, if you assemble the shelf-box all at once, it will be difficult to attach it to the bottom of the tabletop. My solution is to create a subassembly of the shelf-box top and both sides. Once they are joined in an upside down U shape, it's easy to screw that into the underside of the tabletop (see step 12). At that point, you can set the shelf-box bottom into place and attach it as well (see step 13). To begin, place the top panel top-side facing down on a flat surface, ensuring good alignment of the parts being joined. After applying a bead of glue along its edge, position a side panel perpendicular to it, and hold it in place with a pair of clamps.

step 11 ■ Use 2" (51mm) screws to reinforce this joint. The plywood is soft enough not to require pilot holes, but if you feel more comfortable using predrilled holes, now is the time to make them with a ⅛" (3mm) drill bit.

step 12 ■ To keep it neat inside the shelf-box, countersink the screws that will attach it to the tabletop. Be sure to use 1¼" (32mm) screws here, otherwise you can blow a screw right through the top!

technique how-to
EDGE-BANDING 101

Veneered plywoods allow you to create beautiful objects with a minimum of hassle — as long as you have an efficient strategy for dealing with the plywood edge. The simplest solution is to do nothing at all — for some contemporary designs, leaving the laminate layers exposed creates a raw, beefy detail that is appealing. For more refined work, however, it's necessary to cover the edge, and the easiest and fastest way is to use iron-on edge-banding.

Edge-banding consists of a thin strip of real wood veneer, usually ⅞" (22mm) or 1" (25mm) wide [although 2" (51mm) is available in some stores], bonded to a layer of heat-activated adhesive. The banding is available in most major wood species and is sold in rolls that measure 8' (2.4m), 25' (7.6m), 100' (30.4m) and 250' (76.2m). Most home centers only sell rolls up to 25' (76.2m), which may meet your needs, but if you have a large project or en-vision yourself doing a large amount of edge-banding, I recom-mend buying larger rolls from a hardwood lumber distributor. The cost savings is usually considerable — I can buy a 100' (30.4m) roll at a lumber store for only a couple of dollars more than a 25' (7.6m) roll at a home center. One hundred feet (30.4m) may sound like an absurd amount of edge-banding, but you'll probably use more than you think, and it never hurts to have extra on hand for future projects.

Here are a few tips for easy, smooth edge-banding:

■ Precut or tear all the strips you need and put them in a pile where you're working; (this keeps the process moving.)

■ Line up one edge of the strip with one edge of the piece you're banding; this cuts the amount of trimming in half.

■ Use an ordinary household iron set at the hottest temperature. It doesn't damage the iron, so you can borrow one from home. However, I used to get into trouble because I kept forgetting to bring ours back — three dollars at a thrift store ended the strife, plus at three dollars I could afford to replace it pretty readily if, for example, I dropped it on the floor and broke it (I am now on my second thrift store iron for this exact reason).

■ In terms of technique, pass the iron over 12" (305mm) to 18" (457mm) lengths, eight to nine times back and forth at a moderate speed. There is no need to apply heavy pressure. With enough time (just a few seconds) the adhesive melts and takes care of itself.

■ Once the entire strip adheres, I grab a pair of scissors and rub the flat of the blade against the banding to make sure it seats. With scissors in hand, I trim the overhanging ends flush.

■ A sander with 150-grit or 220-grit paper will blend the edge-banding perfectly into the plywood. These grits are both fine enough to grind down the banding without damaging the veneer. Work gingerly at first, treating the veneer as if it were gold leaf, and with practice you'll be able to work more aggres-sively.

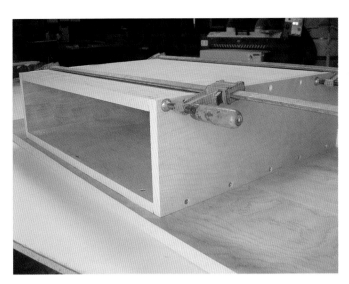

step 13 ■ To install the bottom panel of the shelf-box, place a bead of glue along the edges that will meet the sides. Then simply clamp and screw it into place.

step 14 ■ In order to make the legs splay evenly, the plates must be positioned in a consistent manner. To do this, set the plates on the corners of the tabletop so the short, flat edges (next to the screw holes) are parallel to the edges of the tabletop. The gap between the edge of the plate and the edge of the bottom side of the tabletop should be 1" (25mm) on each side. Screw the plates down using the included ¾" (19mm) self-tapping screws. Though it is probably overkill, I went ahead and epoxied the plates to the tabletop, figuring that if you can easily reinforce an area that might take a beating over time, it is well worth a few extra minutes of work.

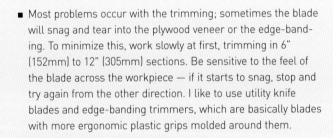

■ Most problems occur with the trimming; sometimes the blade will snag and tear into the plywood veneer or the edge-banding. To minimize this, work slowly at first, trimming in 6" (152mm) to 12" (305mm) sections. Be sensitive to the feel of the blade across the workpiece — if it starts to snag, stop and try again from the other direction. I like to use utility knife blades and edge-banding trimmers, which are basically blades with more ergonomic plastic grips molded around them.

■ Should you edge-band before or after assembly? If you're working on lots of parts that are similar in size, you may as well edge-band them all at once for the sake of efficiency. However, I often assemble and then edge-band (doing so satisfies the instant-gratification component of my personality). Conversely, if you have a small workspace, you may want to edge-band first and hold off on assembly until the last minute (even to the point of prefinishing components). A relatively unobtrusive stack of flat panels can morph into quite a large assortment of furniture once it's assembled.

■ More and more stores are carrying a new peel-and-stick edge-banding, which is definitely quicker and easier to use. The only negative is the cost: For me, it is not enough of a time-saver to justify paying three to four times more than the iron-on stuff. For small projects in which you'll pay only an extra couple of bucks, it may be worth the price.

■ Keep practicing, it may not make you perfect, but it will certainly speed things up.

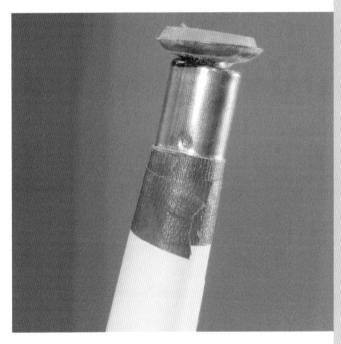

step 15 ■ As a final touch, I painted the brass feet silver. The best time to do this is after the legs have been stained and varnished. Using blue painter's tape and a sheet of scrap paper, simply mask off the leg, then apply a couple of coats of spray paint.

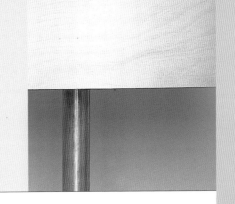

project twelve

table
LAMP

during *this chapter,* I'll try my best to avoid the standard puns about "shedding some light on the subject," but it's hard to limit wordplay when you're as lighthearted as I am.

Seriously, though, lamps are a lot of fun to build because they involve an interesting range of materials. I initially considered a variety of different things for the shade, including cardboard, newspaper and handmade paper, but ultimately chose veneer because I love the warm orange glow it exudes when the lamp is switched on. Once I built a prototype shade, the decision to use copper pipe and a painted silver base came about easily.

This chapter tackles a table lamp that you might find in a living room, den or bedroom, but the concept readily adapts to a taller floor lamp simply by lengthening the vertical structural element — in this case the copper pipe. I'm not sure ³⁄₄" (19mm) copper pipe would support a 60" (1524mm) lamp, but you could have a good time designing something that could — perhaps a few lengths of pipe or some 2×2 lumber?

Because this project involves the installation of an electrical fixture, you must work carefully and follow the manufacturer's instructions to the letter. With only two electrical connections, the job is pretty straightforward, but better to be safe than sorry. Take your time when it comes to running wires and hooking up the light socket.

All in all, I'm sure you'll find this a rather enlightening project.

project drawing front, side, elevation

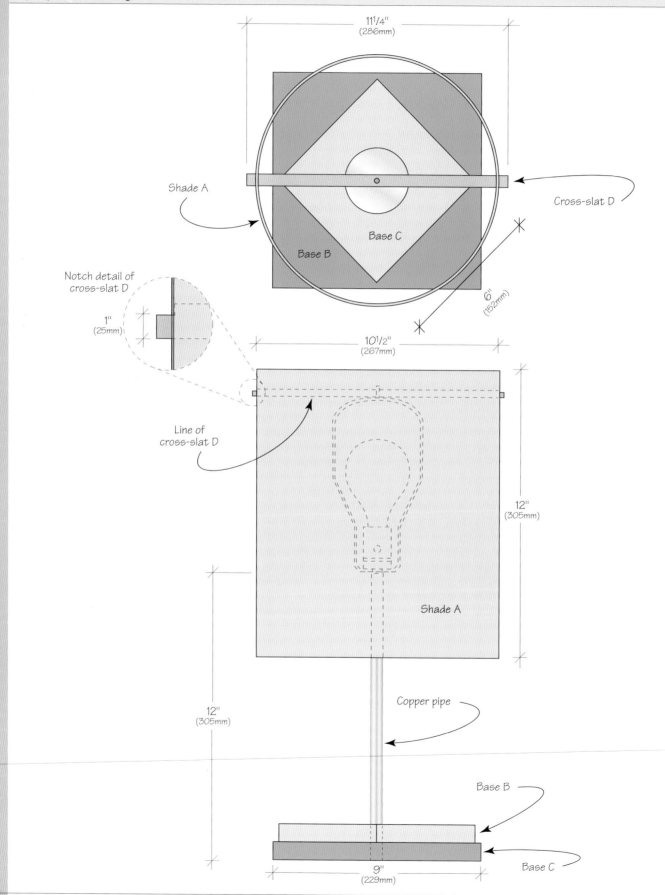

11¹/₄"
(286mm)

Shade A

Cross-slat D

Base C

Base B

6"
(152mm)

Notch detail of
cross-slat D

1"
(25mm)

10¹/₂"
(267mm)

Line of
cross-slat D

12"
(305mm)

Shade A

12"
(305mm)

Copper pipe

Base B

Base C

9"
(229mm)

cutting list inches (millimeters)

REFERENCE	QUANTITY	PART	STOCK	THICKNESS	(mm)	WIDTH	(mm)	LENGTH	(mm)
A	1	shade	paper-backed birch veneer	veneer		12	(305)	33	(838)
B	1	base	plywood or MDF	¾	(19)	6	(152)	6	(152)
C	1	base	plywood or MDF	¾	(19)	9	(229)	9	(229)
D	1	cross-slat	scrap hardwood	¼	(6)	¾	(19)	11¼	(286)

hardware & supplies

- ▪ 1 Westinghouse Make-A-Lamp kit 70268

- ▪ 1 Westinghouse Steel Lamp Nipple 70603

- ▪ 1 Westinghouse Locknut 70172

- ▪ 1 12" (305mm) copper pipe [¾" (19mm) inside diameter, ⅞" (22mm) outside diameter]

- ▪ 1 copper pipe cap (same dimensions as above)

A

B

step 1 ▪ Trim the veneer for the shade to 33" × 12" (838mm × 305mm). Use the sharpest utility or X-Acto blades you can find. I like to use a new blade when I start a project like this, just to ensure smooth cuts. For long, straight cuts, lay down a metal straightedge and cut slowly and carefully. A framing square also works well for this. The blade may wander from the straightedge. To prevent this, make the first cut without applying too much pressure on the knife. This creates a shallow groove that's easy to follow on a subsequent pass. A sharp blade will penetrate the veneer in two passes, three at the most. The veneer shade rolls into a circle and is held in place with tabs on one edge inserted through corresponding slots on the other. Make the tabs 3³⁄₁₆" (81mm) wide and ⅝" (16mm) long. The tabs on the top and bottom of the shade are set in ⅝" (16mm) from the edge. Lay them out with a ruler and pencil. If you're hesitant about making freehand cuts, you may want to practice first on scrap veneer or posterboard. Once the tabs are cut, round their corners slightly so they put up less of a fight going into the slots.

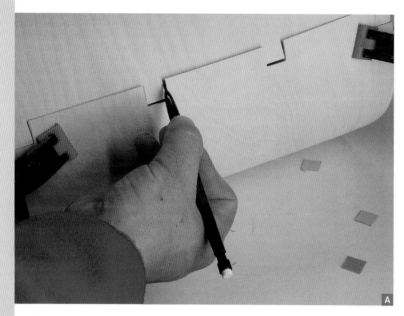

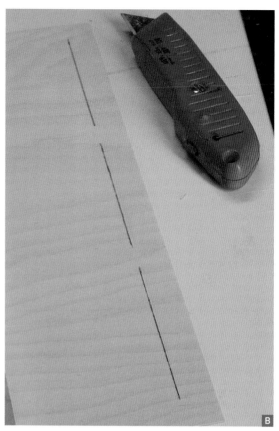

step 2 ■ To cut the slots, roll up the shade and clamp or tape it into place. Mark the locations of the slots from the tabs to provide the most accurate layout possible. The slots will conform to the tabs exactly as they are, not as they're theoretically supposed to be. As an option, you could also layout the slots with a ruler as you did for the tabs and avoid the need to roll up the shade.

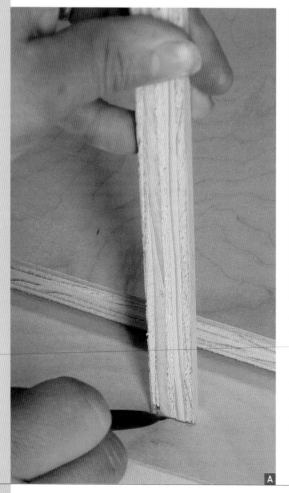

step 3 ■ The veneer is pierced by a 11¼" × ¾" × ¼" (286mm × 19mm × 6mm) wooden cross-slat, which allows the shade to hang on the lamp fixture. Drill a ¼" (6mm) hole in the slat's center for this purpose. You'll need to cut two slots for the cross-slat to run through. It is easiest to cut the first one prior to assembling the shade. Mark the size of the slot directly from the cross-slat, positioned 1" (25mm) down from the top of the shade. Trace the end of the cross-slat and cut it out with an X-Acto blade. The fit should be tight enough to allow the slat to move but only with some effort. A sloppy fit may allow the shade to spring out of shape.

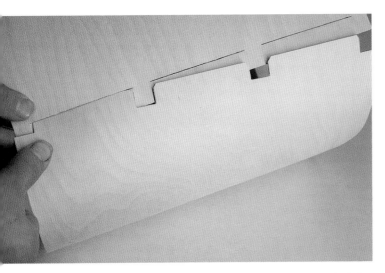

step 4 ■ When you assemble the shade, it may put up a bit of a fight. This is a good thing. Widen the slots a bit only as a last resort. An ideal fit requires no glue. The harder it is to put together, the tighter the joint will be on the completed project.

step 6 ■ To construct the base, use two 9" and 6" wide (229mm × 152mm) squares which you can cut to size using whatever method is available to you. In a well-ventilated area (ideally outdoors), spray paint the tops of the squares silver. I like the look of the raw plywood edges and the way their natural wood color corresponds to the shade, so I took care not to get paint on them. You can sand off any overspray once the paint is dry.

step 5 ■ To lay out the second slot for the cross-slat, insert the cross-slat into the slot and push it all the way down. Make sure the shade is round and the slat bisects the circle into two equal halves. Then simply trace the slot and cut it out as you did in step 4. Push the cross-slat through both slots, and the shade is finished.

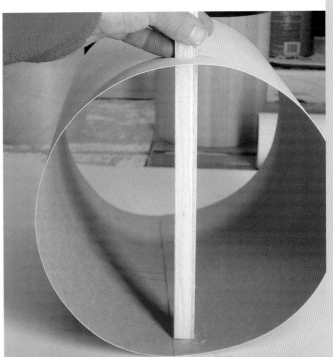

step 7 ■ Locate the center of each square by laying a ruler across the diagonals and marking the intersection.

step 8 ■ Drill the holes in both squares using a ⅞" (22mm) spade or Forstner bit.

step 9 ■ Cut a notch into the bottom square for the cord to pass through. You could also use a router table to do this, but I used my table saw. Position the fence so you cut exactly at the center of the square. Feed the square until you can see the saw blade through the ⅞" (22mm) hole. Then shut off the saw and wait for the blade to stop. By shuffling the fence an ⅛" (3mm), you can create the width you need — three passes worked for me.

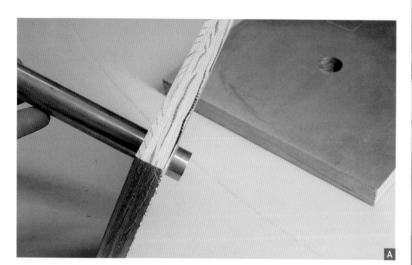

step 10 ■ To assemble the base, put the pipe through the top square. Let ⅜" (10mm) of pipe protrude below it, as this allows room for the cord to run out in the bottom square. After pressing the two squares together (I like to offset the top one 45° to the bottom), screw the squares together (from underneath) using 1¼" (32mm) screws.

step 11 ■ Drill a hole into the copper pipe cap. Use a ¹³⁄₃₂" (10mm) or a ⁷⁄₁₆" (11mm) bit.

step 12 ■ Time to install the light socket, begin by running the cord through the base and up the pipe. Turn to the copper pipe cap and the lamp nipple (the threaded hollow tube): insert the nipple through the hole in the pipe cap and tighten a nut above and below the cap so the nipple is fastened securely. Only about ½" (13mm) of threads should be visible above the cap. Pull the exposed wires through the cap/nipple assembly and wedge the cap onto the pipe — it will be a tight fit and shouldn't require further securing. Finish wiring the socket per manufacturer's instructions.

night
STAND

this piece has a fun, vintage look to it and works equally well as an end table or a nightstand. Structurally it consists of a simple box held up by a symmetrical pair of boomerang-shaped legs. I had originally considered an A-shaped leg with a horizontal crossbar but decided against it because I prefer the more open side. Also, this way it has the benefit of allowing the parts to nest, making for a more efficient use of materials. During the design stage, I often make decisions based on an efficient use of materials. One of my pet peeves is creating weirdly shaped scraps that I'll be hard-pressed to use in the future.

A great way to modify this piece is to add a drawer. If you choose to use metal drawer slides, take a look at the File Cabinet project for tips on installing drawers and slides. If you'd like to go with a quicker and less-expensive option, you might build a drawer box that fits almost snug inside the opening [about ⅛" (3mm) narrower in width], and glue down two strips of ⅛"-thick (3mm) masonite hardboard upon which the drawer will slide back and forth. It isn't fancy — I call them "poor man's drawer glides" — but it does allow the drawer to slide very smoothly. You'll want to install a back or some sort of stop that the drawer will come to rest against so the drawer doesn't push through the back side of the opening.

project drawing top, front, elevation

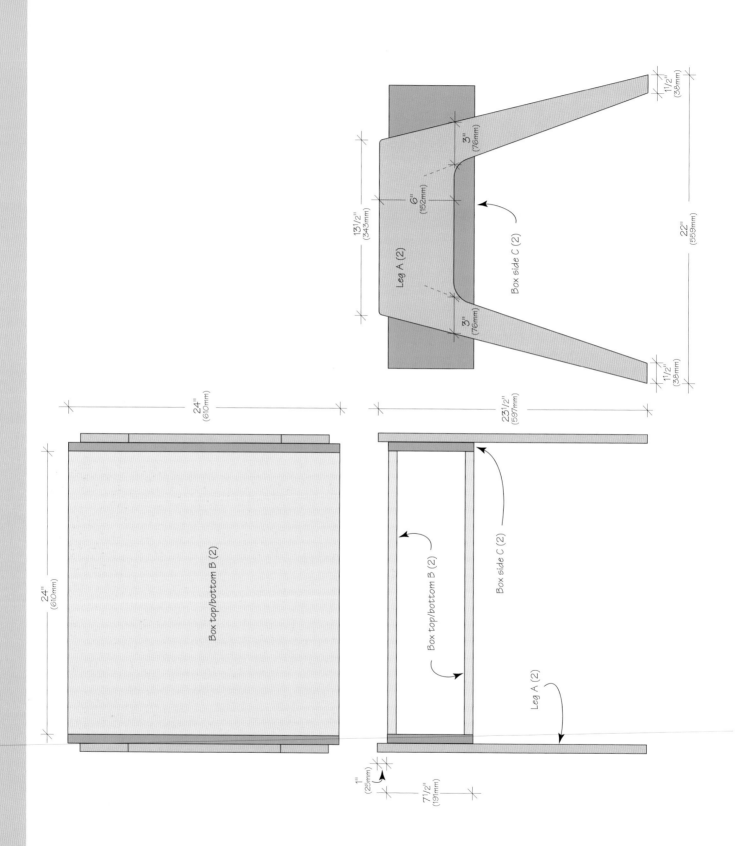

cutting list inches (millimeters)

REFERENCE	QUANTITY	PART	STOCK	THICKNESS	(mm)	WIDTH	(mm)	LENGTH	(mm)
A	2	legs	veneered plywood	¾	(19)	6	(152)	20	(508)
B	2	box top & bottom	veneered plywood	¾	(19)	24	(610)	24	(610)
C	2	box sides	veneered plywood	¾	(19)	7½	(191)	24	(610)

hardware & supplies

- ■ 8 No.10 biscuits
- ■ 18' (549cm) iron-on edge-banding
- ■ 24 1¼" (32mm) pockethole screws
- ■ 8 1¼" (32mm) drywall screws
- ■ 4 rubber bumpers for feet

step 1 ■ Draw the leg onto a piece of ¾" (19mm) plywood and cut with a jigsaw. I like to use maple, which I get a great deal on, although birch looks almost identical.

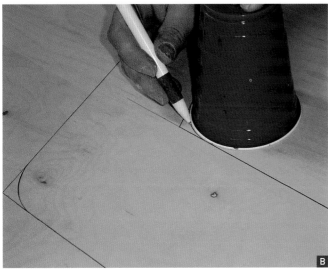

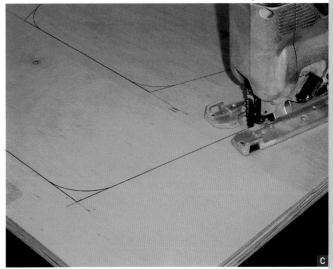

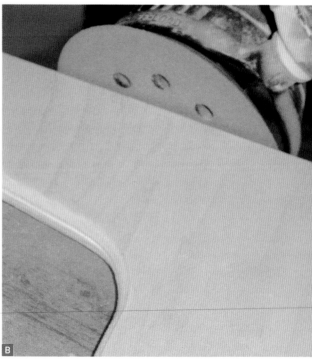

step 2 ■ I even out any irregularities in the cuts with some careful sanding. I recommend using a belt sander for the long flat spots on the outside of the legs, a random orbit sander for inside and sanding drums chucked into a drill for the inside curves.

step 3 ■ Use the first leg as a pattern for the remaining leg. Trace, cut out and sand it smooth as well.

step 4 ■ Once the leg assemblies have been sanded, rout the edges with a ¼" (6mm) roundover bit. This small detail makes a huge difference in the finished leg. Then sand the legs smooth using a random orbital sander.

step 6 ■ The main body of the nightstand consists of a hollow box. You could use a few different types of joints to fasten the sides to the top and bottom: biscuits, pocket screws or plugged screws. I used pocket screws.

step 5 ■ Some iron-on edge-banding is required and now is the time to do it. Start with the top edges of the two side panels. Then apply the edge banding to the front edges of the sides and top and bottom panels. For specific tips, see the "Edge Banding 101" sidebar in the Coffee Table project.

step 7 ■ With the top panel in the pocket-hole jig, cut six pocket holes along its side edge, then turn the panel 180° and do the opposing edge. Make sure to drill the holes on the bottoms of both the top and bottom panels so the holes won't show on the finished end table. Use glue and screws to attach the top panel to the sides.

step 8 ■ Use clamps to hold the bottom panel in place and attach it to the sides.

step 9 ■ The box is screwed to the legs from the inside of the box. To position the box, use a framing square to make sure the distance from the bottom of the box to each foot is the same.

TIP ■ legs

You can also construct this piece using 1½"-thick (38mm) legs. Cut out four legs and glue two of each together to make thicker legs. This is purely an aesthetic choice but one you might want to consider.

step 10 ▪ Apply glue to the inside faces of the legs where the box will be positioned and attach it using six screws per leg. Apply the finish of your choice. Then you can attach little rubber bumpers to the feet of the table legs to protect your floors from scuffs.

TIP ▪ jigsaw cuts

Some jigsaw cuts in the plywood will run across the grain, causing the edge of the veneer to chip. To minimize this, use a brand new blade and, just as importantly, set the jigsaw on its least aggressive setting. Move the saw very slowly. If you still have problems, use a sharp X-Acto or utility knife to prescore the pencil line.

clearly superior
BOOKCASE

plexiglass sides give this versatile bookcase a decidedly modern look, and as an added bonus, they keep it reasonably lightweight and therefore easy to move from house to house or from room to room. The 2' × 2' (61cm × 61cm) frame is surprisingly sturdy, and it goes together so quickly you might want to buy extra materials and build more than one.

The most practical way to modify this design is to change its dimensions, which basically involves two variables: the amount and size of the stuff you need to store and the size of the bookcase's prospective location. Sometimes this last variable trumps the first one, although it is all a matter of personal preference. In my home, there's a bookcase that runs right to the ceiling, as well as a couple of short, wide ones. The tall one maxes out the storage potential afforded by the high ceilings in my home's downstairs, and the shorter ones had to fit below the windows in the dining room. If you know you'll be moving to other homes, it's a good idea to build to dimensions that are most likely to work in a variety of settings. Or, if you really just love a particular set of proportions, there is something to be said for simply building what you like and worrying about finding a place for it later.

If you're not into the look of the Plexiglas, you can use other material you like as a skin for the sides and shelves: painted or stained ¼"-thick (6mm) plywood or hardboard would work just as well.

project drawing top, front, elevation

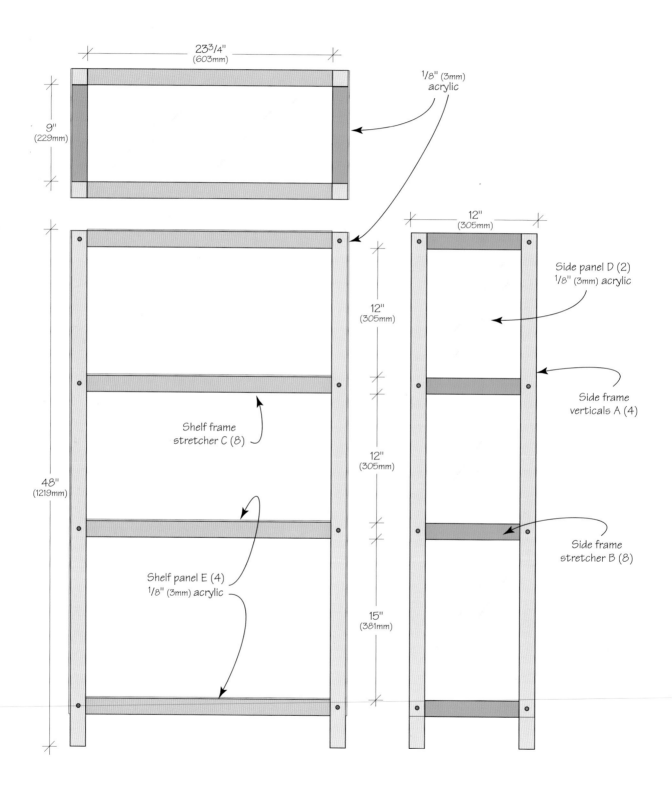

23³/4" (603mm)

9" (229mm)

1/8" (3mm) acrylic

12" (305mm)

Side panel D (2)
1/8" (3mm) acrylic

12" (305mm)

Side frame
verticals A (4)

Shelf frame
stretcher C (8)

12" (305mm)

48" (1219mm)

Shelf panel E (4)
1/8" (3mm) acrylic

Side frame
stretcher B (8)

15" (381mm)

cutting list inches (millimeters)

REFERENCE	QUANTITY	PART	STOCK	THICKNESS	(mm)	WIDTH	(mm)	LENGTH	(mm)
A	4	side frame verticals	2x2	1½	(38)	1½	(38)	48	(1219)
B	8	side frame stretchers	2x2	1½	(38)	1½	(38)	9	(229)
C	8	shelf frame stretchers	2x2	1½	(38)	1½	(38)	23¾	(603)
D	2	side panel	Plexiglas	⅛	(3)	12	(305)	45	(1143)
E	4	shelf panels	Plexiglas	⅛	(3)	12	(305)	23¾	(603)

The 2x2s can all be cut from 5 @ 2"x 2"x 8' (51mm x 51mm x 244cm) with negligible waste.
The acrylic panels can all be cut from 2 @ 24" x 48" (610mm x 1219mm) panels with negligible waste.

hardware & supplies

- 32 3" (76mm) screws
- 40 ¾" (19mm) screws
- 4 threaded leveling feet

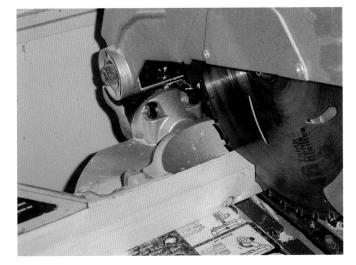

step 1 ■ Start by cutting some 2×2s to length for the sides of the bookcase. They will basically go together like a ladder. You'll need four pieces at 48" (1219mm) long and eight at 9" (229mm).

step 2 ■ The distance between the top 2×2 and the second one down will be 12" (305mm) — I call this the first shelf bay. Position the 9" (229mm) horizontal stretcher there and mark its location so you can easily put it back in place (it will get moved around shortly). As you lay out out the wood parts, be sure to choose the best faces and orient them to the most visible side. With dimensioned framing lumber, doing so makes a big difference — pieces of wood will often have a very ugly face and a surprisingly clean one opposite it. The distance between 2×2s in the second shelf opening will also be 12" (305mm), and the bottom shelf opening will be 15" (381mm).

step 3 ■ To indicate where to place the screws, I mark the vertical frame member with an X. I do this for all four horizontal stretchers on each side of the side frame.

step 4 ■ With a square, simply transfer the marks to the other 2×2s.

step 5 ■ Use a drill bit with a countersinking head to drill holes into the side frames. It's not necessary to drill into the ends of the horizontal stretchers, since the 2×2s are made of such soft wood.

step 6 ■ Apply a dab of glue at each joint, use some clamps to hold the parts in place and screw the sides together. If a screw gets stuck and refuses to go any further, don't force it — reverse the drill and partially back out the screw, then try driving it again. It may be necessary to repeat this "back and forth" technique a few times, but it always works, and it will prevent the screw head from becoming stripped.

step 7 ■ You should now have two side assemblies ready to be jointed together to create the shelf unit.

step 8 ■ When you counterbore holes for shelf stretchers, make sure you do not hit the screws that hold the sides together. Use two screws at each joint. This allows you to go above and below the existing screw and also is a preventative measure against side-to-side racking. Install the shelf stretchers for both the front and back of the bookcase. At this point the frame is almost done.

step 9 ■ The soft pine is a pleasure to sand if you're used to working with hardwoods. It cleans right up with almost no effort. The important thing is to remove pencil marks and clean up obvious scuffs and dings. You can finish the frame with your choice of products: varnish, oil or paint. I liked the light blonde color of the wood, so I opted for a quick and easy varnish-oil top coat.

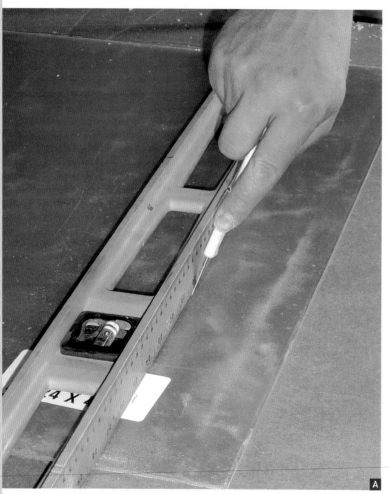

step 10 ■ While the finish on the frame dries, measure for the acrylic side panels. Leave the protective film on while you're cutting the panels to size. My local home center sells special knives that are designed for cutting acrylic, and they proved worthy of their inexpensive price. The blades feature a sharp hook that digs in and scores the acrylic as you draw the knife toward you. Screw or clamp a straightedge to your bench or table so neither the straightedge nor the acrylic can wiggle around. If you pass the knife over each cut about eight or ten times, the acrylic will score nicely. It will then snap in a perfect line when you're ready. I didn't have any problems with cracks or sloppy cuts, and that is probably because I took my time and was, if anything, overly careful. Once acrylic cracks, there is no way to fix it, and I didn't want to make a trip back to the store.

step 11 ■ With the bookcase on its side, place the first acrylic side panel on the side of the bookcase frame. The acrylic is too thin to countersink the screw heads, but it is essential to predrill for the screws themselves. Failure to predrill invariably results in cracks. You'll need about eight screws per side, spaced to correspond with the shelf stretchers. The screw heads will protrude a little but this is not a problem. However, if this bothers you, you can use thicker acrylic and countersink the screw heads. When you finish one side, flip over the frame and set it on some heavy cardboard to protect it. Then proceed to screw down the second acrylic panel.

step 12 ■ After cutting the acrylic for the four shelves you'll find that you're left with a long thin piece to remove. To make sure it snaps evenly and without cracking, flip it over and score the back side as well. This extra precaution works well for such a small piece. The acrylic shelves are attached in the same manner as the sides. You'll note that the acrylic is not fully supported at the ends. I didn't see this as a problem, as it is only a 9" (229mm) span, and even when I loaded the acrylic up, it seemed quite secure. But if this bothers you, you have a few options: You could use thicker (and more expensive) acrylic, you could run a lengthwise stretcher under each shelf, or you could buy longer pieces of acrylic and notch out the corners so they cover the horizontal stretchers in the side frame as well.

suppliers

All of the projects in this book are made using ordinary materials that are readily available at most hardware stores and home centers. Because I am a modern design junkie, however, and because I am also as cheap as all get-out, I have pounded the virtual pavement and come up with a list of sources offering slightly less common products at great prices.

THE DOW CHEMICAL COMPANY (DOW BIOPRODUCTS)
2030 Dow Center
Midland, MI 48674
800-441-4369
www.dow.com/bioprod
■ *Woodstalk composite wheatboard panels*

FERROUS HARDWARE
4404 Westlawn Avenue
Los Angeles, CA 90066
877-FERROUS (877-337-7687)
www.ferroushardware.com
■ *Metal furniture feet and legs*

THE GREEN BUILDING CENTER
1952 East 2700 South
Salt Lake City, UT 84106
801-484-6278
www.greenbuildingcenter.net
■ *No-VOC finishing products*

HARDWARE SOURCE
840 5th Avenue
San Diego, CA 92101
877-944-6437
www.hardwaresource.com
■ *Surface-mounted hinges and more*

HOMESTEAD FINISHING PRODUCTS
P.O. Box 360275
Cleveland, OH 44136-0005
216-631-5309
www.homesteadfinishing.com
■ *TransTint water-soluble dyes*

HOME DECOR HARDWARE
200 South Franklin Street, #8D
West Chester, PA 19382
877-765-4052
www.homedecorhardware.com
■ *Cabinet and furniture hardware (take a look at the M549)*

IKEA
800-434-IKEA (800-434-4532)
www.ikea.com
■ *Inexpensive contemporary hardware*

LEE VALLEY TOOLS, LTD.
U.S.: P.O. Box 1780
Ogdensburg, NY 13669-6780
800-267-8735
Canada: P.O. Box 6295, Station J
Ottawa, ON K2A 1T4
800-267-8761
www.leevalley.com
■ *Stainless-steel drawer pulls at great prices*

MYKNOBS.COM
217-14 Northern Boulevard
Bayside, NY 11361
866-MYKNOBS (695-6627)
www.myknobs.com
■ *Cabinet hardware (check out the stainless stuff by Siro)*

ROCKLER WOODWORKING SUPERSTORE
4365 Willow Drive
Medina, MN 55340
800-279-4441
www.rockler.com
■ *Tools, accessories, supplies and hardware*

SMITH & FONG COMPANY
375 Oyster Point Blvd. #3S
South San Francisco, CA 94080
866-835-9859
www.plyboo-plywood.com
■ *Bamboo panels and lumber (pricey but very hip)*

TERRAMAI
P.O. Box 696
1104 Firenze Street
McCloud, CA 96057
800-220-9062
www.terramai.com
■ *Reclaimed hardwood lumber*

WOODCRAFT
P.O. Box 1686
Parkersburg, WV 26102-1686
800-225-1153
www.woodcraft.com
■ *Woodworking hardware, accessories, and more*

index

More Great Titles from F+W Publications!

Turf

By Anthony Garay
ISBN 1-55870-761-1,
paperback, 128 pages,
#70714

If you like unique furniture but you're on a budget, use your do-it-yourself attitude and this book to come up with creative yet functional chairs, tables, bed frames, and more. These practical designs require a limited number of tools and are perfect for the first-time designer.

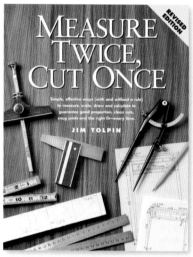

Measure Twice, Cut Once

By Jim Tolpin
ISBN 1-55870-428-0,
paperback, 144 pages,
#70330

Guarantee the right fit every time by mastering the simple, effective ways to calculate, draw, scale, and measure that are taught in this book. You'll learn how to avoid mistakes and how to correct or hide them so that your work perfectly cut, well-proportioned, and precisely put together.

Design Your Own Furniture

By Jim Stack
ISBN 1-55870-613-5,
paperback, 128 pages,
#70555

Learn the mechanics of getting your ideas down on paper and refining them into construction drawings and cutting lists. You'll learn to create a drawing from a photo, re-size furniture plans with easy formulas, standard furniture dimensions and much more!

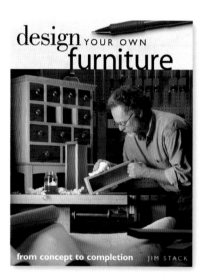

The Woodworker's Complete Shop Reference

By J. Churchill
ISBN 1-55870-632-1,
paperback, 144 pages,
#70579

Think of this as your one-stop-shop for answers to all your woodworking questions and dilemmas. From learning how to sharpen your tools to learning the differences between types of glue, screws, nails, joints and more, this book provides the great foundation every woodworker needs to be successful.

These and other great books are available at your local bookstore or online supplier.